FOREX TRADING FOR BEGINNERS

Mastering the Art of Currency and Commodity
Trading Easily

(A Step by Step Guide to Making Money Trading
Forex)

Susan Schumacher

Published by Andrew Zen

Susan Schumacher

All Rights Reserved

Forex Trading for Beginners: Mastering the Art of Currency and Commodity Trading Easily (A Step by Step Guide to Making Money Trading Forex)

ISBN 978-1-77485-143-2

Legal & Disclaimer

The information contained in this book is not designed to replace or take the place of any form of medicine or professional medical advice. The information in this book has been provided for educational and entertainment purposes only.

The information contained in this book has been compiled from sources deemed reliable, and it is accurate to the best of the Author's knowledge; however, the Author cannot guarantee its accuracy and validity and cannot be held liable for any errors or omissions. Changes are periodically made to this book. You must consult your doctor or get professional medical advice before using any of the suggested remedies, techniques, or information in this book.

Table of Contents

Introduction

So what is Forex? Have you heard of it? A quick search online will most likely give you the following definitions: "Foreign Exchange", "any type of financial instrument that is used to make payments between countries", "refers to off-exchange foreign currency transactions. The term can also refer to some on-exchange transactions as well", "simultaneously buying one currency and selling another", "(forex, FX, or currency market) is a worldwide decentralized over-the-counter financial market for the trading of currencies", and "the market where one currency is traded for another. It is one of the largest markets in the world".

Those definitions can be pretty self-explanatory but in a nutshell, Forex or Forex trading is the buying and selling of currencies and you can make money from that if you know how to get it done right.

If you happen to be planning to venture into Internet marketing or try online jobs as either alternative or extra source of income, you might want to try Forex trading. In fact, a lot of people in the whole world are eyeing this type of online career. Why they do that and why you should try it as well is explained in the following paragraphs.

Now that the question - what is Forex? - has been answered and clear to you, the next thing you, as a newbie, need to learn is how it works. If you do study the whole Forex trading process, you will understand why so many individuals would like to take a shot with this job. One known reason is that doing Forex trading is quite convenient compared to other online jobs (you don't have to write, you don't have to advertise, you don't have to create a website, etc.) and offline work (you don't have to take orders, you don't have to clean glass windows, you don't have to check electrical wires, etc.) as well. Most Forex trading systems can be run with little or no supervision at all because of those automated software and Forex robots. You can now spend some more time with your family if that's what you want.

Although Forex trading can be convenient, that doesn't necessarily mean it's that easy. Some traders find it great to have a convenient yet challenging task. Sure, it's automated and all that but a wise Forex trader or Internet marketer knows that in order to make the most out of this Forex trading system, one should not just rely entirely on automated software, signal providers, expert advisors, Forex robots and the like. Don't let them do the whole job for you because you know for a fact that you can do better than those so-called tools combined. Don't be a lazy ass.

Perhaps one of the biggest, if not the biggest, reasons behind the huge following of the Forex market is the fact that it is such a lucrative opportunity online. If you know what you are doing and you are doing it right, you can earn profits tenfold than your previous job or what you can ever imagine. Here, you can work as much and you can earn as much too. The question now is: what is Forex to you? If you think it's the job you want to pursue then by all means, go for it.

How do people get rich? Other than making savings in every month of doing hard work and determination, people get there by doing investments. The really rich people get involve in the foreign exchange market or better known as the Forex.

So what is Forex Trading and how does it help you earn fast money? Forex is basically about making trading of buying and selling of the currencies in the world. A currency of a country has difference in values than another country's currency and also a value of money today is different than the value of money tomorrow. Therefore, it is from this money value that we can do buying and selling and later earn profits.

In the Forex trading, there are the highest trading currencies which come in four pairs. They are the major business traders in the world, namely the Euro with US Dollar, the US Dollar with Japanese Yen, the US Dollar with Swiss Franc and the US Dollar with British Pound. It has an amount of over $1.9 trillion being traded daily, making the Forex Trading as the largest financial market in the globe. However global this money trading is the Forex trading works without having a physical location and not even there is a central exchange. It runs within a huge network of banks all over the world, corporations and individuals who does trading of a currency for another. Whatever the time is, there will have trading going on in different parts of the world. Thus, unlike the domestic stock markets that only operates on working hours, Forex currency trading operates in a 24 hours a day basis. As long as every country involves in the forex market trading, the market will open all day.

In the earlier times before Forex is introduced and widely used by many, currency trading is difficult to enter because of high barriers. The foreign exchange market could only be accessed by the retail investors through banks that do large amounts of currency transactions for the purpose of commercials or investments. That makes only the large banking organizations and institutional firms that could trade in forex. Then, in 1971, the exchange rates were let to float freely and have made the trading volume increased tremendously. Up until today, the forex market is used by importers and exporters, multinational corporations, speculators, international portfolio managers, long-term holders, and day traders to do their payments for all kinds of goods and services that make businesses running. They also make transactions in financial assets.

It is well-known by Forex traders that the rule of earning money through Forex is by buying low and selling high. However, there is a trick on earning smart money by knowing the right time to buy and to sell. It is a matter of speculation. Graphs are often used to help traders make decisions. Business trends and strategies are also being released in the news every day. But making decisions for the next step is always by predictions based on the previous performance and activity. The politics of a country and how it is running can also be a good measuring aid for analyzing the currency value patterns. Therefore, to be an active trader with smart guesses, one must be aware of the current issues in the national news of the country.

It sure is exciting if you are able to earn a huge amount of money over Forex. But still, the system can be very complex and it may also be risky. It is recommended that a beginner in Forex reads a lot and finds information before opening an account for Forex.

Just what is Forex, Fx, Foreign Exchange? Only the largest financial enterprise on the planet! With more than $2 trillion changing hands everyday the Foreign Exchange market, Forex or FX market, are all the terms that are used to describe the business of the trading of the worlds various currencies. Engaging in hundreds of times the daily trading that happens on the New York Stock Exchange and having its beginning in 1971 the Foreign Exchange Market is where money is sold and bought freely. Forex has become the largest liquid financial market today. Forex is also a non-stop cash market where you speculate on changes in exchange rates of foreign currencies. Forex operates through a global network of banks, corporations and individuals trading one currency for another but have no physical location and no central exchange unlike other financial markets.

FOREX is a perfect market to invest in, as it is free from any external control and free competition. The Foreign Exchange market place is distinguished from the others because of its high trading volume and geographical dispersion. A trader with sound knowledge of currency trading can earn a substantial profit in the forex market. Along with the knowledge of trading, he or she should have access to a few tools of forex trading. These tools are made to strengthen the confidence of a trader and can prove out to be a great help for a winning currency trading in forex.

A Good Forex trader should also know that trying to trade in the Forex market without a broker could lead to damaging results for the normal trader. Determining a Forex broker is a tough process to maneuver through and for most people, the need for external assistance is vital and necessary. Indeed, it is very important that you do your due diligence when researching any future brokerage firms to handle your financial portfolio. A serious Forex Broker will provide a potential customer with clients that are successful because of using their firm and can attest to the specific broker's qualifications and achiever records. One other factor in determining a sincere Forex broker is the margin of return that is offered. A Forex trading margin used to influence your money and many Forex brokers offer different margins. Determining a Forex broker, who gives a margin of ten to one isn't a very good find so it's worth the time to invest in more research.

In years past, just some banks and large lending and financial institutions were the only entities allowed to utilize the Forex market. That is no longer the case, largely because of the technological advancements and the ability by way of the internet, individuals, government agencies and even brokerage firms now have the ability also to do forex trading on the Internet. With a computer, a keyboard and mouse, you too can now become a forex trader. In other words it does not require a financial degree to be able to trade forex. Learning how is very easy and you will need to learn how, in order to become a successful investor on the Foreign Exchange Market.

Above all you need not be troubled or afraid, this same internet has plenty of websites that can and will give you the opportunity to "Paper Trade" before you ever think of going live.

Forex trading is now quite an acceptable occupation for private individuals. It used to be only available to top financial institutions, but the internet has enabled everyone, even people with a low starting capital, to trade the forex markets. So what makes forex trading so attractive?

Well the most obvious attraction is the earning potential. The amount of money you can make from forex trading is unlimited. The sky really is the limit. If you have a consistently profitable strategy, then you can use leverage to multiply your earnings. For example, if a forex broker offers 1:100 leverage, this means you can trade a $100,000 position with just $1000 and a $10,000 position with just $100.

This means that if you are successful your earnings will grow rapidly. Compare this with traditional share trading where if you wanted to buy $100,000 worth of shares, then you would have to have $100,000 in capital.

Another huge draw is the fact that the forex markets are open 24 hours a day during the week. So you can therefore trade during the hours that suit you. Plus there's the fact that liquidity is always high as currencies are traded in countries all around the world, which means that you will generally not have any trouble getting a large position filled at any time of the day.

Another advantage of forex trading is that it is very easy to open an account with a broker and start trading shortly afterwards. There are many top forex brokers nowadays and a lot of them have excellent trading platforms as well as top of the range charting software that you can use to make your trading decisions.

Charts are one of the key tools for any trader as they are invaluable in helping you to find possible trades. They are useful when trading any financial instrument, but they are particularly useful when trading forex because the price, particularly of the major currency pairs, generally conforms extremely well to technical analysis.

So overall there any many reasons why forex trading is becoming so popular. Of course it's very easy to start trading forex, but it's a lot harder to actually make money consistently from forex trading. This is why I recommend starting off by using a free demo account as this will enable you to become familiar with trading, without risking any of your own money. There is a steep learning curve and it's always best to come up with some form of trading system before trading for real.

Chapter 1: Forex Trading

You're likely to have done a basic forex transaction if you've ever traveled abroad. This involves trading your home currency with the currency in the destination country. This is basically what forex traders do: they exchange their home currency with the currency of another country, then make a profit by reverse trading the transaction if the price changes in their favor.

Forex trading involves two transactions: you buy one currency and sell another. This is why currencies are always listed in pairs. The value of one currency is always expressed as the amount it can buy from another currency.

Let's take an example: EUR/USD = 1.1192. This is the currency rate, also known as the exchange rates. The "base" currency is shown on the left, while the one on right is the "counter", or "quote". One euro equals $1.1192. It means that $1.1192 would be the price to purchase a euro. Alternately, you could sell a euro for $1.1192. You can also reverse the quote to determine the euro value of one dollar. Using the above example, one Dollar equals 0.8935 Euro

A currency quote that goes up indicates that the base currency has appreciated relative to the counter currency (base stronger/counter lesser), while if it falls, the reverse happens (base weaker/counter more). If the EUR/USD currency exchange rate moves from 1.1250 - 1.1260, then it indicates that the euro has strengthened in comparison to the dollar. If it falls to 1.1225, it indicates that the dollar is strengthening against the euro.

You exchange euros for dollars when you make a trade with this currency pair. When the currency that you trade appreciates in value against the other currency, the trader makes money. Let's assume that you purchase 100,000 units, or 100,000 euros, for $111,920. You would make $100 profit if your euros were sold, since they now have a value of $112,000. If the dollar appreciated against the euro (the euro is less expensive than the euro), you would make a loss of $100 as the value your euros would drop to $111 820.

To sum up:

For $111,920, you can buy 100,000 euros (100,000. x 1,1192).

The exchange rate has increased to 1:1202. Your 100,000 euros now have a value of $112,202 (100,000.x (1/1.1202).

Sell your euros to close your position and get $100 ($112,202 – $111,920).

Pip is the measure of the change in value caused by an exchange rate. Pip refers to the smallest possible price change that a currency pair can make. One pip equals 0.0001 if the exchange rate can be quoted up to four decimal points. If the EUR/USD exchange rates are currently at 1.1120, and then go up to 1.1130 it is said that it has moved up 10 pip.

A trader can open two types of positions depending on how he perceives the market's direction. If he thinks that the currency's price will rise, he can open a "long" trade, in which he will purchase a currency pair. He can also open a "short", which means he will sell the currency pair if he thinks prices will fall.

A short position is when currency is sold at the current exchange rate to borrow it from the broker. The trader will purchase the currency from the broker to repay him, and keep the difference as his profit. This type of trading is very profitable but it comes with very high downside risk. Short-selling should be avoided.

What is the Forex Market?

The forex market differs from other financial instruments like stocks in that there are no central exchanges such as the New York Stock Exchange and the Nasdaq. This is because trading takes place on the internet. Forex is traded "over-the-counter" which means that traders can trade with one another online via computer networks. Forex brokerages typically deal with traders who place orders and then buy and sell currencies for them. Because they trade only for themselves, rather than for an institution or company, individual traders are called "retail" traders.

Forex traders can trade with brokers anywhere in the world. This means that you can trade any time of the day or week. Trades can be initiated with a Tokyo broker, and then you can move to New York or London with a broker. You can trade forex while you work, or even in your spare time after work.

The forex market's unique feature is that prices are determined solely by market dynamics, which is the fluctuation of demand and supply for a specific currency. Because of uncertainty about the UK's economic future, market participants began to sell their pounds to offset the British pound's depreciation. Because of the constant market changes, the forex market doesn't experience bullish or bearish markets in the traditional sense.

Forex History

The gold standard was the foundation of the forex market as we know it today. Before this, international financial transactions used silver and gold as payments. These precious metals' value fluctuated due to fluctuations in supply and demand in the commodities markets.

This was addressed by the gold standard, which ensured currency convertibility. Every government guaranteed that each unit of currency could convert into a certain amount of gold. A dollar was equal to one ounce of gold. There was a standardized system for currency exchange.

The gold standard required that governments maintain large gold reserves because these were necessary for currency exchanges. This system was broken when major European countries began large-scale military operations. They printed more money to pay these projects than they could back with their gold reserves.

The Bretton Woods system was created by the Allies to fill the void left after the fall of the gold standard. The Bretton Woods system was created in July 1944 at a meeting in New Hampshire. This event drew more than 700 representatives from various Allied countries.

The system saw the dollar replace gold as the main global reserve currency. It would also mean that it would be used in international transactions. A method of fixed exchange rates was established. The US dollar was the only currency to be backed by gold. The creation of three international organizations to oversee global economic activity led to the creation of the International Monetary Fund, International Bank for Reconstruction and Development (better know as the World Bank), and the General Agreement on Tariffs and Trade (whose implementing organisation is the World Trade Organization).

The US ended up running a series balance of payments deficits as it tried to fulfill its requirements of being the reserve currency of the world. The US had exhausted its gold reserves by the end of the 1970s, and was unable to support all the dollars held in reserve at various central banks. In 1971, Richard Nixon, the then-President, declared that the US would cease to exchange gold for dollars in foreign reserves.

The international financial system changed from one that had fixed exchange rates to one that used floating rates after the collapse of Bretton Woods. This meant that exchange rates could now fluctuate on the market rate and not be determined by governments.

The conditions for current forex markets were already in place at this point; however, there was still a small number of market participants. These are:

These central banks are responsible for the implementation of the fiscal and monetary policies of their home country's countries. These banks are often responsible for maintaining the country's foreign currency levels to help them achieve specific economic goals. These banks often look to the markets for help in adjusting the volume of their foreign reserves.

Large financial institutions. These institutions use the interbank marketplace to transact and often buy and sell millions in dollars and other currencies. These transactions are often credit-based. Larger banks with better credit relationships can command higher exchange rates. These banks can trade at higher prices and make money in the forex markets.

Hedgers. These are international businesses and organizations that purchase currency using futures contracts in order to lock-in favorable exchange rates for the future. If a Middle East company wants to purchase US steel for a future construction project, it will need to have enough US dollars to make it possible. The company might enter into a futures agreement for dollars to ensure that the exchange rate is favorable.

Speculators. These people speculate on the fluctuations in the currency exchange rate to make large profits. George Soros is a well-known speculator who bet that the British Pound would lose value. His wager netted him $1.1 Billion in one day (September 16, 1992).

However, not all speculators are successful. Nick Leeson, who used futures contracts to speculate on the Japanese yen, was a big loser. His losses cost the Barings Bank more than $1.4 billion and eventually led to its collapse. It was then bought by the Dutch bank ING.

Retail speculators were unable to participate in forex markets until recently due to the lack of a communications infrastructure that would allow them to directly deal with market makers. The internet allowed individual traders to trade currencies and has seen this group grow in importance and size. To accommodate them, so-called retail brokers are also being created.

There are two types of retail brokers: dealers/market makers and brokers. The brokers seek out the best prices for their clients, and act as their agents on the markets. Market makers, however, are the principals in transactions with retail traders and determine the prices they will accept to trade at.

Chapter 2: Pros And Cons Of Trading Foreign Currencies

Pros of Trading Foreign Currencies

First, the foreign exchange market is largest market in the world and is, therefore, very liquid. A trader can easily transact currency at the prevailing exchange rate.

Second, the foreign exchange trader can earn from exchange rate fluctuations due to the volatility of the market. Although highly risky, he can generate profits from his trading activity.

Third, the foreign exchange market is open 24 hours every day, except weekends. Trading of foreign currencies occur all over the world. The foreign exchange trader can choose the time he wants to trader but the market has the greatest liquidity during those times that operating hours of various markets overlap.

Fourth, trading foreign currencies has the cheapest trading cost. The spread, which is "ask price" minus the "bid price", is the trade cost brokers charge per transaction.

Fifth, some brokers offer a margin account, which is trading account used to obtain a larger position with less money. The foreign currency trader can afford to enter a larger position through leveraging. However, this type of account is very risky because the trader can easily lose his capital and may even be required to add additional money to his account.

Sixth, the trader can short sell a currency. This means that he can trade foreign currencies even if he does not own them. The foreign currency trader sells a currency that he does not have in his position. He buys back the same currency at a lower price to earn profits from the transactions. This strategy of short selling is profitable only when the price particular currency pair is falling.

Cons of Trading Foreign Currencies

First, trading foreign currencies is highly risky. A trader must know that he can lose a lot of money in trading. Thus, it is important that he trade only what he can afford to lose.

Second, the trader must be careful about dealing with fraudulent brokers. He must deal only with legitimate and reputable brokers. He must learn to weed those unscrupulous ones when he picks the best broker to serve his needs.

Third, the trader must have a good working relationship with his broker, recognized by a regulator and of good standing. In Australia, he can source his broker from the Australian Securities and Investment Commission. In the US, his broker must be from the National Futures Association or the Commodity Futures Trading Commission.

In the UK, the trader must ensure that his broker is from the Financial Conduct Authority. In Japan, he can source his broker from the Financial Services Agency.

In Singapore, his broker must be from the Monetary Authority of Singapore. In Hong Kong, the trader can source his broker from the Hong Kong Securities Futures Commission. In Canada, he can choose his broker from the Investment Industry Regulatory Association of Canada.

Using Leveraging

Leveraging is a strategy used by traders to earn more money with little capital. A broker can offer a margin account to his experienced traders and brokers for them to trade more foreign currencies. For example, a 50:1 leverage ratio, means that the trader only has to keep 2% margin in his account. A trader can trade at most $50 to every $1 he has in his margin account.

If he has $1,000 and he can trade at 50:1 leverage, the trader can trade a maximum of $50,000. If his $50,000 trade results to his advantage, he earns that amount of money. Otherwise, he loses the same. He has to ensure that he keeps his account from falling below the minimum limit because the broker can sell the open positions to recover the money.

Chapter 3: Foreign Exchange Risks And Benefits

The Good and the Bad

As we have already mentioned, factors like the market's size, volatility, and global structure have all contributed to its rapid growth. Investors can place large trades in this highly liquid market without having to affect any exchange rate. Forex traders have access to large positions due to the low margin requirements of most brokers in the industry. A trader can control a US$100,000. For example, he or she could put down only US$1,000 upfront and borrow the rest from their forex broker. The leverage is a double-edged sword. Investors can make large gains when rates change favorably, but they are also at risk of massive losses if rates go against them. Many speculators find the forex market attractive despite the risks associated with foreign exchange.

It is the only currency market that is open 24/7 and has decent liquidity all day. It is a great market for traders with a job, or just a hectic schedule. The chart below shows that the major trading hubs can be found in many time zones. This eliminates the need to wait until the opening bell or the closing bell. Other markets in the East open as soon as the U.S. trades close, making it possible for traders to trade any time of the day.

Time Zone	Time (ET).
Tokyo Open	7:00 PM
Tokyo Close	4:00 am
London Open	3:00 am
London Close	12:00 PM
New York Open	8:00 AM
New York Close	5:00 PM

The forex market offers more excitement for investors than trading equities, but the risks are higher. Forex market leverage is extremely high, which means large gains can quickly turn into devastating losses. This can easily wipe out a majority of your account within minutes. All traders need to be aware of this fact. Forex market traders react quickly to new information, which can lead to sharp movements in the price of a currency pair.

Although currencies aren't as volatile as equities in percentage terms (where stocks can lose large amounts of their value within minutes of a bad announcement), volatility is caused by leverage in the spot markets. If you have $100,000 invested and are using 100 to 1 leverage, then you own $100,000 capital. If you invest $100,000 in a currency, and it moves 1% against your currency, the capital's value will drop to $99,000. This is a loss of $1,000 or all of your capital. A loss of 1% in stock value for a $1,000 investment would be a loss only $10. Before you dive in to the forex market, be aware of the risks.

Differences between Forex and Equities

The forex and equities markets have a significant difference in terms of the number traded instruments. There are fewer forex traders than there are equities traders. Forex traders tend to focus on seven currency pairs. These include the four majors (EUR/USD), USD/JPY and GBP/USD; and the three commodity pairs (USD/CAD/AUD/USD; NZD/USD). The other pairs are simply different combinations of the same currency, also known as cross currencies. Currency trading is easier because traders don't have to pick from 10,000 stocks in order to find the best value. Instead, they just need to "keep up" with the economic and political news from eight countries.

Sometimes, the equity markets can experience a slump that causes activity and volume to drop. It may become difficult to close and open positions as a result. An equities investor cannot make a profit in a declining market unless they are extremely creative. Because of the strict rules and regulations surrounding short-selling in the U.S. equity market, it is very difficult to do so. Forex, on the other hand, offers both the possibility to profit in rising and falling markets. Each trade involves buying and selling simultaneously so short-selling is inherent in every transaction. Forex traders do not have to wait for a market uptick to be allowed to take a short position, unlike the equities markets.

Margins and leverage are high due to the forex market's extreme liquidity. In the equity markets, it is impossible to find low margin rates. Most margin traders in the markets require at least 50% of the investment as margin. Forex traders only need 1%. The commissions in the equity market are higher than those in the forex market. Traditional brokers charge commission fees in addition to the spread and fees to the exchange. Spot forex brokers charge only the spread fee. For a deeper introduction to currency trading, see the following:

Chapter 4: The Basics Of The Forex Market

Faith, Currency and Gold

If anyone discovers that I have a love for economics, I usually get a cold or confused response. The reaction all comes form the sentiment that economics could not possibly be interesting, but I believe this is merely because economics is often framed incorrectly. So much of modern economics is thought to be extremely mathematical, and while this is certainly true, economics wasn't always this way. At one point it was more about the study of how humans that don't know each other interact. It is the study of relationships that form around a center of money. I start with this concept because as you begin to trade in Forex, it's important to understand both how the Forex market works and how we came to rely on this system. Understanding these fundamentals have helped me grasp the interplay between countries and has improved my trading overall.

The global Forex markets as we know them today are very different from how currency prices were determined just fifty years ago. You know that Forex markets control the pricing of different currency, but before the currency system countries relied on a gold backed system. There are some that would claim a gold backed system is better than what our economy currently uses, and while there are some merits to this system, our current global economy is far better at handling financial crisis due to a key change in the monetary system of most large economies. The gold system was merely adopted first because of the rarity of gold, and because it is inherently an easy system to understand.

For a moment, consider a piece of currency that you have on you. Whether that note is a twenty dollar bill, or merely a quarter in your pocket, ask yourself; what gives this coin or bill value? It's a simple question but one that is actually quite complicated in the abstract. Before the current financial system the value of your dollar was merely a placeholder for gold that the United States held. The gold of the United States was essentially disturbed around the country through the form of their minted currency. The economy of a country was therefore highly dependent on that nation's supply of gold. If you think back to your history classes in high school and middle school, you may realize that much conflict over the last millennia had roots in obtaining more gold from foreign powers or new land that had not been claimed. This system is simplistic in how it works – it's fairly simple to realize that the currency in hand supplements gold, but it also makes for a lot of difficulty in terms of currency conversion.

For centuries the best way to convert currency was not to go through a government institution, but rather to go through large banks that issued their **own** currency. This currency was a note that allowed traders to use their hard earned money across multiple nations. The banks that ran this system profited immensely, as they were providing a much necessary service that government institutions were simply not handling as well.

The question about what gives your money value is simple in terms of the gold standard, but we can see problems in terms of generating real wealth on a level of nations, and also that exchanging currency was highly problematic, often requiring third parties to handle currency exchange through their own intermediary currency. Today's system is far better, but the answer to the question of valuing currency has changed greatly. In simplest terms, the currency that you have on your persons is valuable simply because you think it is valuable. There is no gold backing your dollar bill; it cannot be exchange in value of any precious metal (dollars used to be exchangeable for gold). The value of the dollar is a collective agreement across the world economy that the dollar is worth something. Understanding this premise that currencies today are largely based on a faith based system, you can start to see how modern currency exchange works.

There's a reason I asked about the value of the US dollar specifically; it is the currency that all other world currencies are traded in. Meaning that if you want to buy Euros or Chinese Yuan, you will be making a transfer in US dollars. From this initial transfer, we have the Forex markets starting to take shape. As currency is traded back and forth, the respective volume and demand of currency is what shapes their value, along with the interaction of various national banks and institutions that can change the money supply. For example, the US dollar's value is based on three inputs: one, that the dollar inherently has value as a tradable item and is recognized across the world. Two, the dollar's value is based on its trading volume and how in demand it is relative to other world currencies. Three, the Federal Reserve has the authority to print money, and this will reduce the value of individual dollars through inflation. Through these three inputs, partially based on faith, the rules of supply and demand and the whim of a government body, we have our modern Forex system.

For your part, you will be making money off of the fluctuations in currency. We'll be getting into the specifics of how currencies are traded, but to give you a simple idea of how you will make money, let's work with a simple example. Suppose that you were to go on a trip to Europe – anywhere in the Euro-zone that accepts the Euro. Before your trip to Europe, you decide to exchange some spending money so that you go shopping and go out to eat. This transaction is an example of a currency pair, in this case the USD/EUR currency pair. If you decide to exchange 500 dollars to Euros, you would currently get 463.59 Euros. The rate of transfer here was 0.93, meaning that for every 1 USD you were provided 0.93 Euros. On the way back to the United States, you realize that you made all of your purchases through your bank card, and that the total amount of 463.59 Euros are still in your possession. You decide to exchange this money back for US currency on your way back to the United States. The transfer of 0.93 has changed, and is now 0.91, meaning for every US dollar you receive 0.91 Euros in return. In this case, the USD has decreased in value relative to the strength of the Euro. When you make your exchange back you are left with 509.44 USD. That's right; in this trip you managed to make ten dollars simply through the fluctuation in the currency rate.

This simple demonstration shows a lot of the specific ways in which foreign exchange currency works. You always purchase currency as a pair, so you are trading on the strength of one foreign currency versus another. Currency pairs are standardized, as is this one: USD/EUR. As the ratio increases, the value of the USD goes up and the Euro goes down. As the ratio decreases, the Euro gains in strength and the USD depreciates. This small-scale example is exactly how Forex works – you make a bet on a currency, hold that currency for some period of time as the price exchange changes, and then sell that currency when you are able to make profit. There are many ways of determining the ideal currency pairs to buy into, but regardless of the strategy, the method to profit is always the same.

The Value of Forex Traders

Forex message boards are a great place to reach out to other traders and learn information about the markets. It can be difficult to find the most useful information on these boards, and some questions certainly come up more often than others. One of the most common topics on these message boards pertains to the value that traders grant to Forex. When you think about what the role of a Forex trader is, it is hard to come away with the idea that they are anything other than speculators. This term, 'speculators' has a negative connotation to it, and I wanted to clarify a bit where the value in the economy comes from with Forex trading.

I gave a simple example of how you can make a profit through Forex with the exchange of dollars for Euros and then back again. The change in the conversation rate was precipitated by the supply and demand of each currency on the Forex market; meaning traders were responsible for the ten dollars of profit in this currency exchange. Why they happened to increase the value of the Euro versus the dollar is where the traders' real value comes in; they are setting the exchange rate for more than your trip, they are also determining the price of imports and exports in a country. In this example, it became cheaper for Europe to purchase items from the United States, specifically because their currency now grants them more USD per a single Euro. This change in their purchasing power allows for more output from the United States because their products are more competitive on a global scale. All of this is due to the work of currency speculators working in their own interests. By trying to determine the value of a currency in the future, all Forex traders work together to set the market rate for currency exchange, and in turn facilitate global trade by setting fair prices for exchange.

If the value that you offer by trading on Forex is still not clear, I want to leave you with one last thought, the power of markets. Imagine if it was the single responsibility of someone to determine the world's currency prices. This would be an immensely difficult job, as it would be up to a single person to determine values based on so many inputs that his or her job would be nearly impossible. When dealing with so much information that could influence the price of a currency, you need thousand of people working in coordination and sifting through all of the different factors that could determine currency prices. The point is that the work of the collective that individually is working in their own self interests, provides a better value for currency prices than any government body or single entity working to regulate the market. The value of the individual trader is that they are added to this collective of information that is determining the value of the currencies across the market.

Chapter 5: Congressive Trading

Congressive trading is a style of trading, where you have one goal—to make a profit each day. It is not a goal of making a million dollars each day, but rather one where you are looking to stick to your strategy and make a profit based on the entries, exits, and risk management positions you enter.

How to Trade Congressive Style

Start with a skill you are comfortable with. Support and resistance are often the most comfortable trend to trade, where you have proven that you can enter the market, make a profit, and close the position before a loss occurs.

Use this skill to gain confidence.

Set your risk management positions to close before you lose.

Keep your trend or pattern indicators simple.

Remain disciplined.

As you gain confidence in your trades, you are going to make minor changes to your entry and exit strategies.

These minor changes will help you increase your profit steadily over a long period of time, versus increasing it too quickly and losing your profits each time.

Further Steps

In congressive trading, you are going to start out with a modest profit.

You will trade the same currencies each day, based on the daily information you receive from the news and technical charts.

You will become comfortable with the currency pairs and how they move.

As you place trades, you will monitor the indicators for anything that might work against you.

After, you open a position, you will reduce the tight risk management order, to gain a higher profit.

Gaining more Profit

At the start, you need to calculate how much of your capital you are willing to lose on a trade. For congressive trading, you want a modest, "tight stop" in place, such as 10 pips from the price you entered at. You might say, you are willing to lose $100 on each trade, thus 10 pips, is a good stop loss point.

Once you gain confidence, you will move your stop loss back, perhaps 20 pips from the entry point.

The closer your stop loss is to your buy-in, the easier it is for you to close the position, without doing anything. A simple, quick turn of the trend before a breakout occurs can have the position closed and any potential profits kept from your grasp.

Note: Make certain you are using a trailing stop. A trailing stop will follow the price. When the price increases or decreases based on the trend, you can take advantage of the change, setting a trailing stop, so you get some profit in the event the market turns around and against your current position. You will sell out at the price the currency moved to versus the market price it hit.

You still want to set a comfortable profit margin, without getting too greedy. Make sure the acceptable loss is within your parameters.

As you continue to trade, with risk management orders in place, you will build a profit over the long term, versus millions in one day.

For most novice traders, this is a more acceptable method than taking on higher risks with leverage and minimal capital.

Chapter 6: How To Start Trading Forex

There are 3 crucial things required to start trading foreign exchange. These are a foreign exchange broker or FX broker, trading account, and trading software.

The FX Broker

In most countries all over the world, financial markets trading is a government-regulated financial activity, with the exception of cryptocurrency trading. In particular, regulators are very keen on regulating activities such as FX trading in developed countries such as the United States, Canada, United Kingdom, Australia, Japan and the European Union.

When I say regulated, what I mean is that there are dedicated bodies of government that monitor and regulate parties that facilitate this type of activity, in accordance with existing laws. Part of the regulatory process is issuance of authorities or licenses to engage in such activities. In the event of serious violations, regulatory authorities can suspend or revoke such licenses on top of imposing hefty fines and other penalties on violators.

To this extent, one of the most important qualities your FX broker must have is a valid license issued by the pertinent regulatory authorities. If you transact with an FX broker that's unlicensed, your protection is only up to the terms and conditions of your contract with the broker and nothing more. And often times, such type of protection is worthless.

After shortlisting your potential FX brokers to those with licenses, you'll need to choose the order execution method or model you'll use for your trades. There are only 2 models to choose from: with a dealing desk and without one.

Brokers that have dealing desks are usually called as market makers. They're called that because compared to FX brokers that just provide you access to the forex market, they're the kind that creates markets for you. They do so by giving your real price quotes, hold your money if your trades lose money, and give you some of their own money if your trade is profitable. The simplest and easiest to understand reason for them being called market makers is because they are your only counterparties for your trades. In short, they're your market.

On the other hand, brokers that have no dealing desk accounts can provide you with a much deeper market in which to trade, i.e., real markets composed of many other forex traders. On the flip side, such market depths tend to have volatile spreads and take a significantly longer time to execute orders. With a non-dealing desk FX broker, also called ECN or electronic communication network brokers, your trading orders are processed and posted on the FX market. Instead of just transacting with your FX broker, an

ECN broker gives you access to millions of other counterparties in the FX market.

So, which is better? Many traders prefer trading through an ECN FX broker because of the market depth, which is normally assumed to provide the best exchange rates. Why? It's because there are substantially more potential counterparties to trade with, which means more price competition. And with much market competition come the best market prices.

But is trading with a market-making FX broker bad because of the fact that dealing with just one counterparty heightens the risk of price manipulation and therefore, the risks for not getting good or market-approximating prices for your trades?

If the market-making broker you're looking to trade with is one that's licensed by a strict financial regulatory agency such as the Commodities and Futures Trading Commission (CFTC) in the US, ASIC in

Australia, or the FCA in the United Kingdom, it's probably not a bad idea. The fact that they are licensed means more government protection and less incentives to act against your best interests, i.e., manipulating your funds and charts and co-mingling your funds with theirs.

The final thing you should consider when choosing an FX broker is the speed at which your orders can be executed. Consider the fact that electronic trading doesn't necessarily mean instantaneous trading because there's such a thing as electronic signal delay, i.e., the time for your trading order request to get to the FX broker's server from your own computer to the forex liquidity provider's own servers, and then back to your computer can take a bit longer than expected. And in the forex trading game, speed is crucial - even a delay of a second or two can spell the difference between being able to profit from your trades or miss the boat. So, if you're very particular with speed of transaction, your best bet would be a market-making FX broker. But if you're willing to sacrifice some speed for market depth and better prices, go for ECN brokers instead.

Trading Account

After selecting your FX broker, the next thing you'll need to figure out is the type of trading account to open. Simply put, a trading account is pretty much the same as a debit account maintained in a bank in that it's where you can keep your money stored. One major difference is that your trading account can contain different currencies, depending on what you're trading. Another major difference is that you can use a trading account to - well - trade in forex!

There are many different types of trading accounts available with different FX brokers. But in general, they differ in terms of the required minimum initial deposits, transaction sizes, the amount of leverage you can use for trading forex, currencies available for trading, and other less significant trading features.

In terms of trading sizes for example, some micro accounts allow for trading amounts as low as $10 per transaction only or trading volumes such as 0.01 unit of a lot, i.e., a micro-lot. And in terms of trading leverage, I mentioned earlier that some offer 10 times leverage while others can provide a leverage of 1,000 times! And when it comes to currencies available for trading, some can have as few as 20 currency pairs while others can have more than 30 pairs.

But for every FX broker, there will always be a regular or standard type of account offered to customers. Typically, most of the available currency pairs are available under such accounts and the initial deposit will most likely be more substantial, beginning at the $200 mark. Such accounts will also most likely have modest leverage.

And then there are the VIP accounts that - just like luxury and sports cars - have all of the top-of-the-line features that any trader can ever want such as funding bonuses, rebates, and generally lower or no spreads, among others. The basic principle with premium or VIP accounts is that if you provide a big enough business to brokers, they'd be very willing to customize practically anything about your forex trading with them. It's a high potential win-win situation.

But as a beginner, stick with the most basic accounts first. You can always upgrade as your trades become bigger and more profitable. And regardless of the type of account you'll choose, make sure you read the terms and conditions of your trading account contract with your FX broker thoroughly.

One of the most important features of your trading account that you'll need to properly manage is leverage. As you become more familiar with forex trading and the more forex-related online groups you join, you will eventually come across debates regarding high trading leverage, i.e., is it good or bad? And because FX brokers offer the highest trading leverage among all financial securities brokers, you'll have to be very cognizant of the very thin line that separates responsible use of high trading leverage and abuse. And your leverage determines how much your required margin is.

A Margin refers to the amount of money - also called initial deposit - that you'll need to maintain with your FX broker as a kind of security deposit so you can trade and open positions, e.g., long or short, with different foreign currencies. Usually, a margin is stated as a percentage of your maximum allowed or available forex positions, e.g., 1%, 3%, or 5% margin.

If your account's leverage is 1:20, this means you can trade up to 20 times the amount of your deposit with the broker. Your margin - the percentage of the total allowed amount of your FX positions - is computed as 1 divided by your leverage, which in this case is 1 ÷ 20. Your margin, in this case, is 5%. So, if you want to trade $100,000 worth of forex, it means you'll need to have at least 5% of $100,000 in margin with your broker, which is $5,000.

Margin calls happen when your existing deposit with your FX broker becomes insufficient vis-a-vis the current market value of your forex positions. When your total position's loss reaches a specific point prescribed by your broker, you will need to put in more money to be able to maintain your leverage. If not, your position will be liquidated and you will suffer the actual losses, which can be huge if not managed properly. That's why even if your broker gives you a high amount of leverage, it's never a good idea to maximize your leveraged position, especially as a beginner.

Trading Capital

The next important thing to consider when you start to trade forex is how much money to start trading with, i.e., your trading capital. As with any other high-risk market-based investments, the wise thing to do is limit your initial trading capital to an amount that you're comfortable losing or an amount that you can afford to lose without becoming financially burdened. Forex trading is one of the highest-risk forms of investment that can provide potentially very high returns but also make you lose your entire trading capital - or even more if you leverage too highly.

And considering that you'll most likely lose money in the beginning of your forex trading journey, limiting your initial trading capital to an amount you can comfortably lose is the wisest thing to do. Just consider that amount as your tuition fee for learning something that can help you make a lot of money eventually.

Trading software

The final important aspect of your forex trading is trading software or platform, which is what you will be using to trade foreign currencies. There are many kinds of trading software or platforms and in some cases, brokers can provide multiple platforms for its customers. However, their functional differences aren't much and they all tend to have all the key features, financial instruments or currencies for trading, a chart that gives you real-time information on your position's current market prices, and an interface that allows you to monitor your key account information such as available margin, position balances, equity, and current trades.

So even before you start trading, give yourself a day or two to become familiar with the broker-provided trading platform or software. Doing so will allow you to focus more on your actual trades instead of having to split your focus between how to use your trading software and trading itself. And when it comes to optimal market timing, nothing is more important than focus.

Chapter 7: Basic Chart Patterns

Chart patterns are another area of technical analysis. It is well-known that investors purchase and sell securities and currencies for thousands of different reasons. Some do it based on fundamental analysis while others do it based on recommendations. Others follow their gut instincts and emotions. Traders take profits or cut their losses short. This is the eternal economic principle of supply and need. The price action will reflect which of these two dominant forces, and the price will continue to move in the same direction or reverse. Chart patterns, which are visual expressions of supply and need, often reflect price changes before they occur. Prices rise when demand is dominant, and fall when supply is.

Chart patterns can be divided into two categories: continuation and reverse. A reversal pattern is formed when a trend shows signs of reversal and stops. A continuation pattern is often formed when price moves in the opposite direction to its original trend. These price patterns can be seen on a variety of time frames, from monthly charts to minute charts. Let's take a look at the basic patterns in both these groups.

Reversal patterns

Before a trend changes, reversal patterns are created. This is a smart way for traders to close any positions they may have opened in the opposite direction to the trend. They will also search for the right moment to trade in the opposite direction.

Head and shoulders (bearish), or inverted head and shoulders, (bullish).

The Head and Shoulders pattern is common at the end of an upward trend. It indicates that prices will fall if the price pattern is valid. This pattern is composed of three peaks: the left shoulder, the head (the highest peak), and the right shoulder. Ideally, the left and right shoulder should be roughly equal in size and length.

The first peak is located on the left shoulder. The price will often fall after the peak is reached. The price rises and pushes upwards by removing the previous peak (or head) from its place. The price drops again, reaching the same level as the decline from the left shoulder, although it may be lower or higher. The price rises, but not to the top of the head. Price starts falling again. The right shoulder forms at this point. The neckline is formed when the low of left shoulder and low of head form. If the price falls from the right shoulder to the neckline, and then continues falling, the pattern can be considered valid and it is said that a downtrend has begun.

How to trade it

Most traders place a sell stop order below the neckline. Your order is automatically opened if the neckline is crossed. Then you follow the current trend. The distance between the top of the head and the neckline is the minimum target. This is generally accepted. We can assume that the price of breaking the neckline will be 500 pips if that distance is reached. This chart will help you to understand. You can place a 500-pip take profit order, which is the minimum target you expect to hit. You can also try to get more but you should then increase your stop loss (trailing) so that your profits are protected.

Here is an example of the eur/aud daily charts. This pattern was formed in just 4 months. The pair was already in an uptrend prior to the formation of the pattern. It reached its first peak on December 27, 2013. (left shoulder). It collapsed, and it formed the low on 13 January 2014. It then rallied and formed the low on January 13, 2014. It fell again, and reached the lowest level on February 13, 2014. The neckline of this pattern is created by connecting two low points. The second low price rose but didn't reach the previous high. It formed the right shoulder, and then fell through the neckline. The distance between the neckline and head was approximately 840 pips. Therefore, our target price for selling eur/aud was approximately 1.4140 (minimum target). Make sure your stop loss is no more than four times your target profit.

Chart no 6. Chart no 6.

A downtrend is the same. An inverted head or shoulders is formed when a downtrend is over. This indicates that a bearish tendency is over and that a bullish one is about to begin. The rules of formation are the exact same except that the pattern is inverted.

Double top (bearish) /double bottom (bullish)

A double top is a bearish pattern that occurs at the end of an upward trend. It is composed of two peaks which are almost equal.

A pattern must have a prior uptrend in order to form. The pattern's first peak should be its highest point. The price begins to fall once it has reached that peak. Bullish price action takes place after a while. The price rises to its' prior top but fails to break it. The second peak has been formed. The second peak may be slightly lower than or slightly higher than that of the first peak. The price then reverses and returns to the previous peak low. This should be a support. If support is broken, a downtrend is initiated.

The distance between the first peak and the lowest point of the first decline after the peak would be the minimum target.

Most traders wait for support to break before placing a sell order. This is the best way to trade double top. We can only tell if the support has been broken convincingly. You can set a stop at 10-20 pips below the support level. If price moves there, your order will be opened.

Here is an example of a double-top on a weekly chart with the eur/usd pair.

It is evident that the first peak was attained in the middle of April 2008. The second week of May 2008 saw the low and support. The price rose again, and the second peak occurred in July 2008. The price crashed through support, and a massive downtrend began in eur/usd. The distance between the first peak and support was approximately 740 pip. This was our minimum profit target. It was easily achieved in a month. The price crashed further.

Chart no 7. Chart no 7.

You could have placed a sell stop at 1.5270-60 level, with a stop loss target of 100 pips, and a take profit target 700 pips. This would have resulted in a very nice profit.

Double bottom patterns should follow the same rules, except that they are inverted.

Continuation patterns

When a trend slows down for a while and then resumes, Continuation Patterns are formed. These patterns are shorter and tend to have a stronger breakout in the direction of previous trends. Flags and triangles are the most well-known patterns in this group.

Triangles

There are many types of triangles, but all share the same basic principle: narrowing range. A pattern must have at least two lower highs, and two higher lows in order to be valid. This is a clear indication of a narrowing range. This can be linked with trend lines or converging lines, which gives rise to a triangle shape.

The price must reach a certain point in order to continue the trend. If the trend was upward, price would rise to the highest point of the triangle. If the trend were down, we would expect the price to fall through the lowest triangle point.

The base of a triangle, or the highest and most low points of the triangle, is often used to calculate the target move for the minimum possible after a break. This is the expected move size from the breakout point.

Let's take a look at the triangle that formed in eur/usd downward trend on an 8-hour chart. It lasted for a very short time. The pattern lasted from August 8th, 2014, to August 18th, 2014. It was approximately 100 pips at the base, which was our minimum target for a break lower. The range of the triangle narrowed on the 18th August and the move lower started. The low point (4 on the chart) at 1.3350 was broken. Price moved easily over 100 pips in just two days.

Chart no 8. Chart no 8. Bearish triangle

How do you trade the pattern?

Trade the pattern by placing a sell order below 4 points of a chart pattern. A buy order would be placed if the triangle is bullish and formed following an uptrend. The stop loss should be 50 pips. Minimum take profit order must be 100 pips. This doubles the size of a stop-loss order. Your automatic sell stop order will be opened once the price reaches the target. This could happen within one day.

Flags

Also, flags can be continuation patterns. These patterns usually appear when the market consolidates following a major move, and then they continue for a while.

Before consolidation (short-term range) can begin, a flag must contain a sharp movement. This is what creates a kind of flagpole. It is a distance between the previous point at which a move began (support or resistance depending on whether trend was up/down) and the current support/resistance point. This is the highest or the lowest point in a current flag pattern. The price then forms a rectangular, sloping channel that looks like a flag. If the previous move was upward, the sloped channel would be downward. Conversely, if the move was downward, the sloped channel would be upward. Trend lines can be used to clearly see the slope of a channel or a flag.

How to trade a Flag

A bullish flag eventually breaks upwards, and the price moves through the channel's upper trend line. Conversely, a bearish flag breaks downwards when the price passes through the channel's lower trend line.

If you wish to trade a bullish flag, you will need to place a buy order above the flag's upper trend line. Your order will be opened once the price reaches that level. You can then start making nice pips if the price moves upwards. Keep your stop at a tight place. You could get around 50 pips.

You must reverse the order of events if you wish to trade a bearish flag. Place a sell stop at the flag's lower trend line. Your order will be opened once the price reaches this level. You can then make a lot of pip. Your stop loss should be kept at 50 pips.

You can usually determine the area where you want to take profits by calculating the flagpole's size and adding that number of pips on to the breakout point.

Here is an example of a bearish flag which developed during a downtrend in the eur/usd pair. It took around one week for the flag to form so it was only a brief respite before the downtrend returned. The flagpole measured around 300 pips long and the pair traveled that distance in a single day after the channel trend line broke. Simply place a sell order at the 1.1550 level, maybe 10 pips lower. You also had a 50 pip limit loss and a 300-pip profit target. You would have gained 300 pip profit and the trade would have been in your favor. It took just one day to trade a bearish flag pattern.

Chart no 10. Bearish flag pattern

Risk management

People tend to carry a survival kit with them when they travel. It's strange that new traders don't have the necessary knowledge to become successful traders. The ebook covers some of the key aspects to success in Forex trading, but not all.

This chapter will focus on one. You will fail as a trader if you have the rest. Risk management is the one thing that will allow you to succeed and survive.

It is not enough to just make money. You also need to protect it.

Making money and saving money are the two most important things in a business. You won't be able to survive if you don't make enough money but you spend more. Your business will fail. In the event of a disaster, you will need to keep some of your earnings.

This is also true for investing in currencies. To be successful in the market, you must not only make money but also protect your capital. Statistics are a good place to start. Around 80 percent lose all their currencies invested within one year. They lose most of it in the first months of trading. Why? There are many reasons why they do this, but the most important is that they place too high a risk on their capital.

Do not risk your entire capital in a single trade

There are many stories of traders who risked their entire capital in one trade hoping to make a profit, but ended up losing everything. I can offer you a piece of advice if you are expecting to do the exact same thing: go to the casino and try your luck at roulette. It doesn't make a difference whether you gamble at a casino or risk it all.

Protect your capital because it is what you will make money with. Your money is your tool to make money. If you don't win, you will lose the tool that allows you to make money. This is something you can't do. One thing you should remember is that before you can learn how to make money with currencies, you must also learn how protect it.

Remember that there will be good and bad days. Sometimes you will experience a "losing run" when there are a lot of trades in a row that you lose. You will survive these streaks if you don't risk too much.

It is not an option to use a stop-loss.

A stop loss order can be a great way to reduce your risk. A stop loss order is essential to avoid trading that could lead to financial disaster. Markets can crash in seconds due to a variety of fundamental events. Stop loss may be the only thing that will allow you to survive.

What is the recommended stop-loss percentage?

You must be willing to take risks if you want money. But the problem is how much. Investors agree that 2 percent equity is the maximum amount you can risk on one trade. Even if you plan to open multiple positions, it is important to ensure that your total risk percentage for all trades does not exceed 2 percent.

When your trade is in profit, you can move your stop loss orders.

You can also protect your money and capital by moving your stop loss order once your trade is profitable. It is impossible to predict whether your trade will reach your profit target. It is wise to adjust your stop loss once you reach a certain level of profit. Let's suppose you have 100 pip of profit. Although you expect the price to continue to move further, it is impossible for you not be wrong. In the event that price falls against you, you can move your stop loss order to lock in profit. To make sure you don't lose anything, you can lock in 50 pip profits if you are making 100 pip profits.

I hope this helps you to see the importance of capital protection. This lesson will save you money and help you trade more successfully.

Chapter 8: Faqs On Forex Trading

It is obvious that you will have a few questions pop up when you take up a new topic. In this chapter, we will look at some of the most common questions that get asked on the topic of forex trading and answer them to help you understand it better.

Is the forex trade lucrative?

Yes. Forex trading is a lucrative business. You will have the chance to make a lot of money if you understand how exactly to play. We looked at the basic concepts and strategies that you need to employ when you choose the currencies to trade in. Once you choose the best pair, you can easily make a lot of money from it. You have to remain alert and attentive, and that will help you in a big way. You can make thousands of dollars a year by indulging in forex trading.

Should I be commerce literate for it?

No. You don't necessarily have to be commerce literate for it. You also don't have to have any relevant experience in the stock market in order to invest in forex trading. You will be able to start from scratch and make it big in the world of currency investments. The currency market welcomes everyone with open arms and does not really discriminate. It will not know who is a beginner and who is an expert and will treat everyone the same way. So don't think of your lack of knowledge or experience as a drawback to trade in the stock market.

What about bid/ ask, spread, etc.?

Bid/ask and spread are all terminologies that you should acquaint yourself with before you start investing. These are common terms that are used across all stock market trades and are not unique to just forex trade. Once you understand what these terms stand for you can easily start trading in forex. You can go through a glossary of all these terms and understand each carefully.

How much money should I invest?

That is completely up to you. When you open an account to trade in forex, the company might ask you to deposit a certain sum. This sum can be $100 or $250 depending on the company. You don't have to use up all of the amount to invest and can allow some of it to remain back in the account. You might have to maintain a certain minimum amount which cannot be used or invested and will make for a buffer in case you are unable to pay for any of the investments that you have already made. There are people who use as less as $10 to make thousands of dollars of profit.

Can I trade on my own?

Yes. You can independently trade in the forex market. You don't have to rely on others to do it for you. It follows a very simple process where you type in the name of the currencies and also type in the amount. Once it is approved, you will be given your currency. You then hold it until you wish to sell it again. You can continue with this process for as long as you like. There is no limit on how much you can buy and sell. If at the very beginning you find it tough to indulge in this process then you can take the help of an expert to get started with it.

Can I trade over the phone?

Yes. You can trade over the phone. You need to call your broker and ask him to buy you the certain currencies. You can also have the currency buying software installed on your phone and use it to buy and sell your currencies. It is really simple and will help you trade in currencies on the go.

Why do the currency prices fluctuate?

There are many factors that contribute towards the fluctuation in the currency prices. There are economic and political causes that affect the prices and cause it to change. There are also other geographic and business-related causes that can cause the currency prices to vary. There is just no telling what will end up influencing the prices of the currencies and will entirely depend on the current events.

Can I have my account funded?

Yes. You can have your account funded by someone else. They will have to directly add the money to your account in order for you to invest it. But you have to show evidence that they have willfully added in the money into your account for you to use in forex. There is no limit on the amount that can be transferred to your account.

Can I withdraw all profits?

Yes. You can withdraw the entire amount that you get as profit from your forex trade. But you might have to leave behind a certain amount that is seen as the minimum balance that needs to be maintained. You have to leave that much behind and ensure that you don't invite any unnecessary fines. Some companies might not even have this minimum balance scheme, and you can easily withdraw all the money at once.

Will I get possession of the foreign currencies?

Yes and no. It depends on the time that you wish to hold the currency. If the time exceeds the 5-day limit, then you might have to take possession of the currency. If you are indulging in intra-day trading, then you will not have to take physical possession of it.

These form the different FAQs that get asked on the topic and hope you had yours answered successfully.

Chapter 9: Forex Trade Psychology

As with any speculative activity, the importance of psychology in currency trading cannot be overstated. People are emotional beings and have evident mental traits that often accumulate in many unique personality types. Also, as marketers gather in the crowd, their overall psychological behavior changes markets and creates highly graphic patterns that stimulate technical analysts.

The underlying psychological factors of a professional's personality are usually emphasized when Forex transactions begin to generate significant profits and losses. Many people experience strong emotions while earning and losing money.

Many researchers have thoroughly studied the psychology of currency trading, usually to determine the type of thinking and personality that are most successful in terms of consistent profit generation.

Many of these researchers have written essential books on the subject that marketers can read to understand their actions better and determine if they can become an excellent professional psychologically.

The discussion on negotiation psychology will begin with a review of the primary personality types, as explained by Dr. Van K. Tharp.

Business psychology or personality types

In his research on psychological trade, Van K. Tharp divides traders into a set of fifteen personality types that can be assessed using the online Tharp Trader test. Each of these personality types has a psychological profile that contains different strengths and weaknesses. Their website provides more details on the subject for the interested reader.

The features that define these fifteen personality types are:

A precise merchant

These buyers are known for their willingness to use detailed analytical processes and keep accurate and meticulous records. Traders with this psychological profile often follow detailed information about the decision-making process in their journal, which generally helps them in future negotiations.

Due to meticulous attention to analysis and record keeping, operators can sometimes fall into the trap of focusing more on these activities than on concluding profitable contracts.

Administrative merchant

This merchant profile is characterized by a tendency to be practical, decisive, and realistic in a commercial approach. An investor usually responds to a changing market environment that can generate profitable transactions. In addition to adapting to different market situations, this type of operator has excellent decision-making skills and can delegate authority when working with others.

Art Seller

Art sellers tend to use intuition and creative thinking more in relationships than other sellers. Thanks to their creativity, art sellers are more flexible and adapt to changing market conditions. However, this trait can be a double-edged sword and cause trouble for a trader if he is emotionally attached to losing trading positions.

Adventurer

This operator profile is known for its open and flexible approach to trading and includes some of the best-known operators. Adventurous investors use their ability to respond effectively to market information. Typically, experienced analysts prioritize data and use it to make the right business decisions. Brave buyers often take significant risks and focus on objective data when making business decisions.

Detailed buyer

A preliminary analytical process characterizes a detailed operator profile before it is launched on the market. Specific investors use logical assessment and careful analysis and often have complex notes about their business and the reasons for it.

However, many traders with this psychological profile may wait too long for closing or closing trading positions, resulting in significantly lower returns.

Merchant facilitator

This type of trader generally takes a sober approach to trade, preferring to trade in a social environment or interact with other buyers. Because of their focus on the social aspect of commerce, these traders usually excel in the sales team or as someone's business partner. Traders who facilitate trade often observe the entire market and negotiate in a resolute and well-organized manner.

A merchant who likes to have fun

A salesman profile who likes to have fun has a fun approach that involves some degree of social interaction during negotiations. Loving Fun Traders usually have positive perspectives that reflect their optimistic attitude. However, due to his optimism and social interactions with other sellers, his emotions may affect his objectivity during negotiations.

Independent buyer

These operators usually use data interpretation and operate independently of the crowd during negotiations. Although his ability to think outside the box can lead to fruitful negotiations, a lack of social skills makes him a bad team player.

An innovative merchant

This type of trader is known for its creative and intuitive approach to information analysis and negotiation. Innovative traders can process large amounts of information and react quickly to the market. In addition to being able to analyze market conditions and respond to them, these traders are usually good leaders and can stand out in the reading.

Planning merchant

This type of trader is usually a competent leader and communicates well in business. They are generally well organized and realistic and effectively make professional decisions. They focus on facts to make sound decisions and can respond quickly and flexibly to new market conditions by developing new systems.

A socially responsible merchant

Such traders are usually loyal to the social values they consider essential and enjoy social life. They seem to be more successful as investors when the trade opportunity matches their values.

Spontaneous merchant

These operators usually think and respond quickly to transactions, even if they do so without thorough prior analysis. They can use planning and problem-solve in their business strategies.

Strategic Merchant

This group of traders usually makes intelligent business decisions based on objective information and develops an appropriate level of competition in their trade-related activities. They are generally considered practical, realistic, well organized, and decisive during negotiations.

Such investors also have a big picture when trading and think quickly in response to market changes. They readily understand difficult concepts and actively learn.

Merchant jointly and severally.

These operators appear to be intelligent, severe and can rely on commercial activities, although they do not have some essential features of the best operators. Therefore, they play a supporting role in a business team or offer to finance more efficient operators.

Value Investor

This type of trader is usually independent and focuses on material rewards, ideas, and business relationships. They can also make the right decisions and see the big picture. If they can overcome emotions and the value system, they can be successful as traders.

Optimal entrepreneurship and psychology of speculation

The emotional and psychological discipline of a successful market speculator has been the subject of many interesting books, such as those mentioned above.

Although not all experts agree, research on this topic indicates several beneficial psychological factors and behaviors people need to be involved in having the best chance of marketing success.

They can be summarized as follows:

• Avoid trying to beat the market. Instead, try to be sensitive to your direction and adapt to it.

• Learn to put greed and fear in the right place. He is afraid when he loses money, reducing short-term losses and desires when he earns money so that profits can flow.

• Avoid trust and excessive transaction risk.

• Don't let injuries damage your confidence and ruin your day, and start perceiving failures as the general cost of doing business as a currency trader.

• Keep a positive attitude.

• Focus on maintaining business discipline and sound financial management practices. Do not change the business plan, whatever the market does. Adjust your outline if necessary, but only when trading positions are closed to avoid impacting the project.

The basic idea here is to examine speculative activities on the currency market as a company. You will win on some transactions and individual transactions, so consider this as part of the trading process. In general, you should always try to manage your company and brokerage funds to stay in the game for a long time.

MASS PSYCHOLOGY AND ITS MEASURES

Many salespeople use mass-market psychological measures to influence their business decisions as part of a business plan. It is said that most of the graphics used by technical analysts reflect certain aspects of mass psychology that are usually repeated.

Some technical traders also use Elliott's theory of waves, which takes into account the psychology of the market. Their movements develop successively in five successive waves, followed by a correction in opposite trends, which usually occurs in three. Waves.

Another popular measure of mass-market psychology is the Market Engagement Report or TOC published every Friday for contracts last Tuesday by the Commodity Futures Trading Commission or CFTC.

The result of this weekly report informs traders of the net value of open positions in each contract where twenty or more traders are in areas close to the disclosure limits set by CFTC and are divided into various categories of traders, including traders and non-TV Advertising. Commercial. Traders.

Traders are those who usually protect their screens as part of their business. On the other hand, non-commercial operators often speculate on the futures market. They consist of hedge funds, financial institutions, and individual investors.

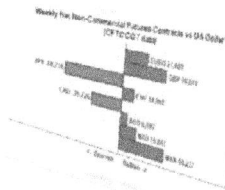

As an example of the data presented in the weekly TOC report, the table in the figure below describes the weekly net results of this report for each of the major currencies traded on the Chicago IMM futures market for non-traders. Commerce.

Many traders use the TOC report to determine the direction and scope of positioning forward currencies in the markets they are interested in. This can be used as a measure of market sentiment to give analysts an idea of the position of large futures traders.

An essential element for traders is how current positions on the list differ from those listed in the previous week. Identifying these weekly changes provides traders with a guide to changing futures markets and options they want to pursue.

For example, when many non-traders position themselves in a certain way, this may indicate that market deterioration may occur as soon as these extreme positions begin to develop. In addition, when TOC positions change from positive to negative, this usually indicates shortening of the market, while a change from negative to positive may indicate a long position in this market.

Chapter 10: Basic Strategies For Beginners

When you want to be successful as a beginner in FOREX trading you have to choose a trading strategy that will help you realize profits and reduce losses. Some traders would choose one trading strategy while others would prefer to have a mix of strategies that would help in determining trades. Strategies include those derived from fundamental analysis and those derived from technical analysis; it is advisable to use strategies from both the two analysis to help you make long term projects and determine when to enter a trading point and leave.

Use of Technical Analysis Trading Strategies

Technical analysis strategies use the price of the security being traded and the volume. The technical analysis strategies help you to know the trend of the price of the security and quality of the patterns formed on the chart; therefore, as a trader, you look for a signal to buy or sell the securities.

Use of Volume Trading Strategy

The volume of securities shows the amount or quantity of securities traded within a given period. When the volume of the securities is high, it means that the market of that security is experiencing high pressure. When it is analyzed, it gives an indication of either a downward movement or upward movement. As a trader you should look at the movement of volume of security that is accompanied by the movement in the price of the security; a price movement that is accompanied by the high volume of security is a good indication of time to enter the trade. For instance, if the volume of the security starts to decline in an upward trend, it means that the trend is about to reverse, and therefore, as a trader prepare to sell your securities. It is good to always look at volume of security traded in terms of, is it decreasing or increasing and is it accompanied by changes in prices.

Identifying a trend might not be an easy thing to do for a beginner trade in FOREX trading. To identify an uptrend, look at the chart and identify the highs and lows of the graph, if you draw a line joining the highs and the lows and the line is drawn inclines or slants to the right, then the trend is an uptrend, and if it is inclined or slants to the left, then the trend is a downtrend. In the upward trend, every low is followed by a high while in the downward trend, every high is followed by a low.

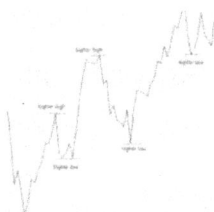

higher high sequence

The use of multiple time frame analysis is another trading, which involves analyzing the price of the security at different time frames. The price of currency changes through different times frames. As a trader studies the changes in prices at different times and determine the cycle; when does it increase and when does it decrease. Also look at the scales in the increase and decrease of the price, which will give you the overall market trend of a particular security. The time frames for study can include analysis of the security during the day and know at what time of the day does the price of the security rise and the time it falls. The weekly analysis involves analysis of the days of the week, looking at each day and establishing the day that records the most increase in price and decrease in price. The monthly analysis involves looking at the weeks in a month, which week registers the highest increase in price and which one experiences the lowest. Is it the first, second, third, or the fourth week of the month? After determining the trend, then it becomes easy to determine the cycle and you can always use the trend in trading. However, it is good to keep analyzing the changes every month, week, and day to ensure that you are not using the trend that does not exist. However, time frames are not restricted to monthly, weekly and daily, you can choose your own time frame depending on you're the type of trader you are.

Generally, there are three types of time frame, long-term, intermediary, and short term frame, but one can have more than three down frames. The recommended number of time frames are three; using fewer timeframes can lead to loss of important data, and time frames more than three can lead to redundant in the analysis. When choosing time frames, choose the intermediate, then choose the short term, which should be at least a fourth of the intermediate period; for example, if a short term frame is 4 days, at least the intermediate should be 14 days, and the long term 56 days. When studying charts, begin your analysis with the long-term because the trend will have established compared to the other time frames and end with the short term frame. The long-term time frame tends to have periodicity such as monthly, weekly, and daily; therefore, you should monitor the economic trends that are influencing the general trend. The economic trend can include consumer spending, deficits in current accounts, and business investment. However, the economic trend causing the long term time frame trend can also change because they are dynamic, and therefore, they need to be checked occasionally. You should also check the interest rate, as it shows the economic health, as it affects the exchange rate; higher interest rates will increase capital and increase returns on investment.

The intermediate time frame is important when using position trading techniques and should be closely monitored when the trade is getting closer to the profit target or the stop-loss point. In the short term time frame, the changes are more clear, and it is during this time frame that you can get an attractive entry whose direction is already known through the analysis of high-frequency charts. The multiple time frame analysis is suitable for beginners in FOREX trading because it is the best way of benefiting from the trend causing the changes.

Fundamental Analysis Strategy

Fundamental analysis concentrates on the fundamental factors that cause the change in market direction. The rationale behind the use of fundamental is that macroeconomic indicators such as interest rates, inflation, unemployment rates, economic growth rate, or political issues that can influence financial markets. The analysis of these microeconomic indicators can be used to make trading decisions. When one of these events occur, and you suspect that it will increase the price at which a certain currency is exchanged, buy the currency and exchange it later, and when you suspect that it will bring the price of a currency down, you sell the currency and wait to buy it later at a lower price.

Use of FOREX Day Trading Strategies

When you are a beginner, and you are interested in FOREX day trading, you can utilize strategies such as daily pivots, scalping, and momentum trading. FOREX day trading is essential because you can enter many trades in a day but before the market closes for the day, make sure that liquidate all the trades.

FOREX scalping is a strategy that involves doing short and quick transactions that allow you to make many profits within the day on small changes in the price of a pair of currencies. This strategy involves minor price move, and it is, therefore, easier to follow compared to large ones. This strategy is highly recommended for beginners in FOREX trading. The trader does a lot of exchanges using the bid and asks price, and within a short time, he or she sells and buys currencies and then exchanges them at a reasonable price to make a profit.

When using the scalping strategy, it is important to consider factors such as time frame, volatility, liquidity or the currency, and risk management. When trading in a more liquid market, you can easily enter and leave large positions, and when trading in a less liquid market, you enjoy trading with larger spreads (the difference between bid and ask price). The two markets are profitable, but it depends on what you prefer as a trader. When it comes to volatility, as a beginner, try to avoid currencies that are highly volatile to reduce the worries of sudden changes in the price of the currency. Generally, scalping is good for beginners, but a risk management skill is required to minimize the losses that might arise.

Fading trading is another strategy that used based on assumptions that if it rises, it will fall, and if it is falling, it will rise; therefore, traders make a decision to buy or sell against the current trend. Although this strategy is risky, it is easy to execute and therefore recommended for beginner traders. It can also fetch a lot of profits if you enter the market at the right point and also leave at the right point because the trader makes a profit at any reversal of the trend. To execute this strategy, you require two limit orders that will be used to minimize losses; a buy limit order below the currency's current market price and a sell limit order that should be set above the currency's market price. Those who engage in fading are known to be high risk-takers who make a large profit. They execute their trade with assumptions that if they buy early, they will take profits, and the currency is overbought, and therefore its price is about to rise up. The daily pivot is another strategy that can be used on daily trading. The trader, therefore, buys with an assumption that he or she will sell in the future at a profit and sells on assumptions that the prices will go down, and you will buy at a lower price than the current one. It is easy to use a strategy that can be mastered to earn profits; however, you should also master the entry point as it will determine how much you get from the trade.

The momentum strategy is also a trading strategy that uses the style of trading. Daily trading is characterized by small price changes to make a small profit, but trade in many currencies to increase the total profit made in a day. However, traders can choose a currency that is strong against the other, with the assumption that the trend in the currency will continue for quite a long time before a reversal occurs. This strategy goes well when it is used together with the trend. This means that before the trader decides to buy the currency, he/she must have observed the trend and with the strength of the currency, concluded that the trend will not change soon. Therefore, he or she buy s or sells the currency, hoping to make some money before the trend reverses.

Market Sentiment – FOREX Trading Strategy

This strategy uses the attitude of the investors towards a given currency or towards the market. Remember that people will behave according to what they feel, and the same happens when making decisions concerning financial markets and the products. When fundamental macroeconomic indicators and other topics that affect FOREX trading are discussed by a group of traders in the market, their reactions determine how they will trade. Therefore, always listen to the opinion of other traders on given topics because they will be reflected in their trades. Again, in a market, every trader has his or her own opinion, but it does not mean that your opinion can shift the market in a particular direction; however, the views and opinions of particular traders can move the market. Therefore, you can trade in the reverse direction when the market is shifted in the other direction. When most traders are buying, you sell, and when they are selling, you buy, anticipating that the reverse will happen soon, and you will get your profits.

As you have seen, one trading strategy is never enough, there are times when a given strategy is more profitable than the others; therefore, be strategic enough to use the strategies interchangeably, using the most appropriate strategy at a given time and in a given situation.

Chapter 11: Fundamental And Technical Analysis

Fundamental Analysis

Fundamental analysis is a financial market analysis method to know the price movements and predict the future outcome of the prices of the asset in the market. Fundamental analysis in forex trading has its focus centered overly on the economy.

The analysis also researches on a variety of factors that affect the forex trade as well as how the elements affect the national currency value. Various factors influence the economy, and these include interest rates, employment, unemployment, GDP, international trade, and manufacturing industries.

In fundamental forex analysis, the price of the may differ from the value of the same asset in the market. Prices may vary because of various factors, and because of the difference in the price and the value of the asset, different markets underprice or overprice the demands for a short period.

However, the fundamental analysists believe that despite the value of the assets being underpriced, mispriced, or overpriced in the short period, and it always goes back to its original correct price after some time. The main objective of any fundamental forex analyst is to get the right price and value of the asset, compare the two, and finally come up with an opportunity to trade.

Fundamental analysis is very different from technical analysis. Fundamental analysis does not pay a lot of attention to the current price like the technical analysis. The fact is that fundamental analysis is not an excellent analysis tool for intraday traders in forex trading. Forex fundamental analysis has many different theories that try to explain it and make it a suitable analysis tool for forex trading. The most common approach is economic theory. This theory attempts to explain that the price conditions should be exchanged when they are adjusted. It summarizes that this exchange should be done according to the local economic factors.

Major Economic Indicators

The economic data in the market shows the movement of the economy of different countries. A trader who wants to invest should be very keen on commercial change. The major economic indicators show the price movements, comparing it to their values giving the traders opportunities of finding new trading chances to invest and profit.

Inflation

Inflation is the balance between the circulation of money in economic growth and distribution. Each country or market has a set level of which the rise can reach. There is a healthy inflation level and unhealthy inflation level. If the economic growth and money circulation in the market are not maintained, the country or any market is likely to suffer from crippling inflation. The balance between the two brings about a healthy inflation. Every economy works very hard on their economies so that the sound economic level can be maintained.

When inflation is high in any economy, supply and demand are disturbed. Supply gets an advantage because there is more than what is demanded. This high inflation affects the currency negatively. The currency drops. Oppositely, when inflation is low- deflation, there is more demand than supply. During this deflation period, money value rises, and the cost of goods go down in the market. It is a strategy that most economies employ but on a short-term basis. If deflation strategy is used long term, it will have adverse effects on the economy. The responsible party will get a hard time stabilizing their economy again.

Gross Domestic Product (GDP)

Gross Domestic Product of a country is the sum of all the monetary value of all goods and services of a given country within a specific time frame. This monetary value of the goods and services must be produced within the borders of that same country. A country's Gross Domestic Product is calculated annually, although there is a possibility of calculating it quarterly depending on the countries policy concerning the GDP calculation.

Gross Domestic Product is the best economic indicator among other economic indicators. Most people think GDP can never be an indicator because it only measures the market value of the goods and services, but they are wrong. From forex fundamental analysis view, when there is an increase in a gross domestic product without an increase in the demand of the products, this constitutes to a weak economy.

Interest Rates

There are different types of interest rates, but the main focus of fundamental forex analysis falls on the nominal and the base interest rates. The central banks of different states set these interest rates. The central bank has to lend money to private banks after creating money. Therefore, the interest amount paid by the private banks on the loans they have acquired from the central bank is called the nominal interest. The nominal interest rate is also known as the base interest rate.

Interest rates balance any economy in the world. It is probably the most reliable economic factor indicator for any forex trader to look at before going into the trade. The interest rates- nominal have a significant influence on the values of the assets, in this case, on the currencies. They also influence other factors like unemployment, manufacturing, investment, and inflation.

Since it is the duty of the central bank control and boost the economy of the country, it makes sure that inflation reaches the country's set level and does not go past that. If it wants to boost the economy of a respective country, it brings down the interest rates. When the nominal interest is down, more private banks will go to the central bank to borrow money while individuals will go to the private banks to borrow money. There will be high production and high consumption correspondently. This act of the central bank will improve the economy of a country but in a short time not a long time.

In as much as interest rates are good at improving the country's economy, it is a poor strategy. The low-interest rates in the markets after a long time will cause over-inflation of cash in the economy and cause an imbalance in this economy. The imbalance caused by this low-interest rate is likely to affect the country for a long time before the economy goes back to normal. Sometimes it paralyzes the country's economy entirely.

However, most of the central banks have a remedy for this inflation. When the economy starts swaying, or after a short period of reducing the interest rates, the central banks increase the scales again. When the interest rates are raised, the money circulating in the market decreases. The private banks will not take loans, and the individuals will not go to the private banks borrow. So, when the interest rates start changing, a forex trader should find his opportunity and make an entry or exit in the trade.

A trader should put in mind that the information released on the economic data is critical. He should carefully consider it, with the forex fundamental analysis if he wants to succeed in the forex trade.

Advantages of Fundamental Analysis

Show the trend of the market price.

Can be an excellent and reliable indicator, especially when it is combined with the technical analysis. It can work out for long term trades.

Technical Analysis of Forex Trading

When price patterns change from one to another, causing a change of prices in the market, these patterns have a specific way of doing so. When changes in price patterns in markets are studied and mastered to help in the prediction of future price patterns, this is now called the technical analysis. Most traders prefer using technical analysis over fundamental analysis. However, some traders use both the analysis techniques. Technical analysts use a different method to analyze the price patterns in markets. The techniques used include:

Chart Patterns

These are patterns where the prices are drawn on charts inform of graphs. When data is drawn on the graph, there is always a repetitive pattern. This pattern shows the movement of the prices in the forex markets. It shows the strength and the weakness of the trade. Some forex traders use the chart patterns as continuation signals or the reversal signals.

The continuous signals contain, triangle, flag and pennant, channel and cup with the handle while the reversal includes, double top reversal, double bottom reversal, triple top reversal, head and shoulders and so many other. There are three groups of chart patterns that traders use — these chart patterns area the candlestick patterns, the harmonic patterns, and the traditional patterns.

The technical analysts using this chart patterns use horizontal lines, trend lines, and the Fibonacci retracement level to find the signals of the chart patterns. The chart patterns show the strengths and weaknesses of the forex market.

Horizontal Lines

These lines are also called sideways trends. These lines connect the lows and the highs in the variables. In this case the prices on the charts. These lines show the price that is below the support level and above the resistance level.

Trend lines

Trend lines are lines drawn on the chart or the graph to show support or resistance. These trend lines are dependent on the direction in which the prices are going in the forex trade. They are also known as horizontal support and resistance. When analysts are using trend lines in the chart patterns, they can see the increase or decrease in supply and demand.

The traders make up their mind whether to invest or not when this increase or decrease occur. When the prices are going up, it is called an upward trend, and the forex traders can sell. When the prices are going down, it is called a downward trend, and buyers can make their entry in the trade.

Fibonacci Levels

These levels in chart patterns exhume the hidden support and resistance. The support and resistance can be hidden due to the golden ratios. The origin pf Fibonacci is from the mathematical proportion, but it acts like the old support and resistance in the chart patterns when the price levels are laid out. The mathematical proportions used in this method is very different from the highs and the lows on the price charts.

Candlestick Patterns

Forex technical analysts use to find the open, high, and low-price levels in the markets (OHL). The prices sought must be of a specific period in the trading session so that a comparison of the trader's behavior during the trade is made against the prices at that particular time. This analysis will help in predicting the future price movement in the forex trade market.

Technical Analysis Indicators

The technical forex analysts use the price action indicator. These indicators include;

The moving average

The moving average indicator shows the averages of prices in a given period. The moving averages display the direction of the market. The moving average helps balance the prices in the market by removing the unwanted prices. This removal helps the trader focus on the trend of the prices in the market. There are four types of the moving averages, namely the exponential moving averages (EMA), simple moving averages (SMA), linear weighted average (LWA), and the smoothed averages.

Bollinger Bands

This indicator is a tool used in technical analysis that comprises of three lines. These lines are plotted positively and negatively but away from the simple moving average of the currency price. These lines are adjustable to the trader's preference. The Bollinger bands help measure the variation degree of prices during the trade. In simpler terms, it measures the volatility of the market in a given period.

Amongst the three lines in the Bollinger, the middle line shows the trend direction of the prices while the upper and lower lines are the volatility lines, also called the volatility bands. The upper and the lower bands are moved above and below the middle band by two standard deviations. This movement of the upper and the lower bands put the price between the two outside lines. This price does not stay here for a long time because it is always moving around the middle line.

The Moving Average Convergence Divergence (MACD)

This price indicator shows the momentum of the market. It shows when the market is doing well or not and the force behind this action. While using this indicator, a signal will always be evident is a market is moving in one direction. The Moving Average Convergence Divergence indicator belongs to a class of oscillators. Oscillators are technical indicators too and shown separately, below the prices in the charts.

Technical analysis has principles that should be followed during the review.

Principle of Technical analysis

Price Moves according to trends

Technical analyses assume that the prices in the trend move according to the trend patterns. The prices move in a bullish trend, bearish trend, and the sideways trend.

All price movements repeat themselves

The theory in this principle called the Dow Theory assumes that the price of a commodity represents its actual value, and it does not have to look at other factors. The principle claim that the prices in the patterns are repetitive and any future price is likely to be the same as the current price.

Advantages of Technical Analysis

Shows the Trend of the Market

Technical analysis shows the traders direction of the market. They can know the time the downward movement of prices and the upward movement, hence enabling them to make to sell or buy at the appropriate time.

Shows the trader Both Entry and Exit points

Timing is essential to a person trading in the forex. Poor timing will cause significant losses, and which will cause the trade to fail. The technical analysis predicts the time for investment for traders. It gives traders the upper hand to know when entering the trade or exit that trade.

Different indicators in technical analysis aids traders get the advantage of knowing investment time early. The candlesticks, moving averages, chart patterns, trend lines, and other indicators help in the calculation of the entry and the exit time in the trade.

Technical Analysis is fast

Technical analysis is fast in giving information about a specific trade. This action makes it quick and reliable to short term traders like the intraday traders who trade in one minute to thirty minutes. In this trade, candlestick patterns are used.

Technical Analysis Gives Adequate Information

Short term traders use technical analysis, swing traders, and long-term traders. Enough information is found in the chart patterns, and forex traders can use this information to their advantage. The traders can pursue their trades utilizing this information and get satisfying returns. More details like the trading psychology, market momentum, volatility, support, and resistance are a portion of the vital information that the technical analysis provides.

Technical Analysis is Cheap

Technical analysis of soft wares is cheap. Some soft wares are free offers from different charting software companies, and they can even be downloaded on mobile apps.

Gives an Early signal

The technical signal traders and investors early on when the time is right to invest. It is like a wake-up call to go in or come in or out of the trade. The correct entry or exit time for traders will help them good gains on their trades.

Chapter 12: Scalping Strategy

The most important thing to remember about this strategy is that it is not for everyone. This is for people who seek to make a profit from the mall market movements. They take advantage of the ticker tape which never stands still during an average market day. This group of people usually relies on the bid/ask screens that they can locate any buy/sell signals as well as to read the supply and demand imbalances. They can even see what the average bid and ask price is. Scalpers usually buy when the demand is up and sell when the supply is up in order to make a profit or a loss that will later balance the conditions that will be returned to the spread.

Sadly, this method is not best in the modern day market due to the electronics for any of the following reasons. First, after the 2010 flash crash, all the order books were emptied out permanently due to the deep standing orders that became the target for destruction that day thus forcing managers to hold them off the market or to execute them into a secondary venue. A second reason is because of the high-frequency trading that is a dominating factor for intraday transactions. This means that the wildly fluctuating data leaves an undetermined market depth interpretation. And finally, a great majority of trades now days take place in what is known as dark pools therefore real time is not reported.

However, even though there are electronics that help in making this strategy harder to be used, there are also ways that scalpers have overcome the challenges with three custom tuned indicators for short term opportunities. Signals that are used for real-time tools are actually used for long-term market strategies, however now they are applied to two minute charts. This works best when a strong range bound action controls the intraday tape. But, they do not work during any periods of confusion or conflict.

Conditions can be seen when they are in place by when the trader gets a whipsawed loss at a great pace which will be present on your profit loss curve. (You can read more about this in **Introduction to Trading: Scalpers** (http://www.investopedia.com/articles/tr ading/02/081902.asp) , **Understanding the Ticker Tape** (http://www.investopedia.com/articles/01 /070401.asp) as well as **The Basics of the Bid-Ask Spread** (http://www.investopedia.com/articles/tr ading/121701.asp)).

Moving Average Ribbon Entry Strategy

The chart above shows a two minute chart which identifies strong trends in which trades can be bought or sold on a counter swing. This is also a warning of an impending trend change which is inevitable on a typical market day. However, this scalping strategy is easy to master due to where the ribbon aligns and points higher or even lower during the stronger trends. Any penetrations that are show signal a waning momentum that will favor a reversal. therefore, should the ribbon flatten out during these swings, the price may crisscross the ribbon frequently. However, a scalper must watch for any realignment because when the ribbon turns higher or lower or even spreads out, there will be more space between each line. Patterns like this trigger a short buy or sell signal. (read more about this: **Market Reversals and How to Spot Them** (http://www.investopedia.com/articles/te chnical/04/031004.asp)).

Relative Strength/Weakness Exit Strategy

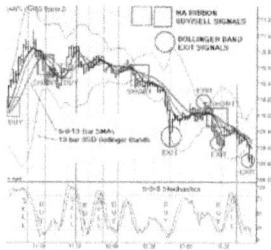

How does a scalper know exactly when they should take their profits or when they should cut their losses? Stochastics as well as Bollinger bands can be used in combination with the ribbon signals on a scalpers two minute chart in order to work with an active market. Any of the best ribbon trades are going to be set up when the Stochastics turns higher from the oversold level or even when they lower from the overbought level. Therefore, an immediate exit will be required should the indicator cross then roll against your position after a good profitable thrust. (You can read more about this on **What Are the Best Indicators to Identify Overbought and Oversold Stocks?** (http://www.investopedia.com/ask/answe rs/121214/what-are-best-indicators-identify-overbought-and-oversold-stocks.asp)).

In order to see when to exit more precisely, you should watch the bands interaction with the price. Band penetrations usually predict what the trend is going to do; either slow down or reverse. The scalping The scalping strategy can not stick around through any sort of retracements. So, the best time to exit is if the price thrust fails to reach where the band is but the Stochastics rolls over.

At the point in time that you are comfortable with the interaction and workflow between all the technical elements, you are then free to adjust any standard deviations higher than 4SD or even lower than 2SD in order to account for the market's daily changes in volatility. An even better idea is to superimpose any additional bands to the chart you are currently using in order to get a broader variety of signals. (You can read more about this technique at **Capture Profits Using Bands and Channels** (http://www.investopedia.com/articles/fo rex/06/bandschannels.asp)).

Multiple Chart Scalping

You can keep track of any background conditions that may impact your performance by pulling up a fifteen minute chart in which there are no indicators. Once you have done this, you can add three lines one of which is used for the opening print and the other two are used for the highest and lowest of the trading range that happens within the first forty five to ninety minutes of your trading session.

While you do this, you need to make sure and watch for price action that happens at those levels because they are going to end up setting up a larger scale two minute buy or sell signals. It is proven that during this you'll find your greatest profit during your trading day when your scalping aligns with your support and resistance levels on your fifteen minute and sixty minute charts or even your daily charts. (There is more information about this on **Trading With Support and Resistance** (http://www.investopedia.com/video/play /support-and-resistance/)).

The Bottom Line

It is proven that anyone who uses the scalping technique can no longer trust any real time market analysis for their buy and sell signals so that they can book multiple small profits in a day. Therefore, they are forced to adapt to the modern electronic environment which uses technical indicators so that the trader can custom tune the very small time frames that are used with the scalping process. (For more, you can read it here: **Scalping as a Novice Trader** (http://www.investopedia.com/articles/ac tive-trading/033015/scalping-novice-trader.asp)).

Chapter 13: Trading Strategies

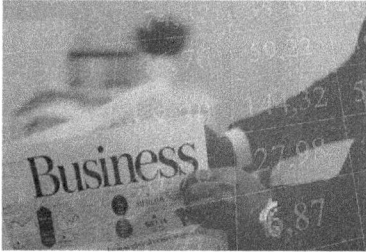

In this chapter, we will introduce you to some of the top Forex Trading strategies which will help you to make a lot of profit with your Forex Trading endeavors. More specifically, this chapter will help you to understand the main three methods top Forex Traders use, especially in the beginning to see amazing results when it comes to gaining profit from the trade. The primary 3 for trading strategies that we're going to talk about is going to be, breakout strategy, moving average crossover strategy, the carry trade strategy. As you know, there are many participants in the Forex Trading industry.

Some of them don't know what they're talking about, where else other are well-versed in this trading industry. After speaking with a lot of professional who have done very well in Forex Trading, we come to you with the top three strategies which will help you to perhaps take your forex trading to the next level. The top Forex traders in the industry, have tried many approaches and have seen success with some and seen extreme failures with others.

Nonetheless, we will guide you with the top three strategies that will help you to see results from the get-go. It is very important for people starting Forex Trading to see results right off the bat, the reason why is because it will help you to build confidence with your Forex Trading Endeavors. As we told you previously, it is essential to see quick results with for trading primarily in the beginning so that the Traders can feel a lot better about their skills. However, do not get carried away with their was also you see in the beginning. If you think you are thus hot shot in trading, news flash for you you're not. You make a big mistake if you keep using the strategies for the wrong reasons, it is essential that uses approach for the right purposes and the right cause. Which is what we're going to teach you in this chapter, so you can finally see the money grow in your bank account. Keep in mind, the first two strategies that we will be showing you are very similar to each other as they are trying to follow a trend. The third strategy attempts to gain profit from the interest-rate differentials, rather than the market situation. People that don't know what trends are, they are necessarily a way for people to determine how the market is going to continue moving on given the overall status.

The trend is essentially a way for the traders to go by the signal rather than actual facts about it, similar to technical analysis which is going by the direction. The good news is that following strategies which require you to look at Trends, can yield you amazing results when it comes to gaining profits. However there are some drawbacks to it, the first one would be it is difficult to stick with it. You have to realize that friends come and go, and the game you'll get from following a strategy which requires you to look at the trends will be short-lived however can he'll do a lot of profit that will help you in the long run. Second drawback of the strategy would be that large friends can be very infrequent, again you have to realize that Trends don't come and go that easy which is why they're called Trends as they come rarely. Keeping that in mind you have to understand that whenever you see a trend, it will be short-lived and it will not happen again in a long time. Third drawback of following a strategy which requires you to look at trends, will not be as frequent. Like we told you previously if you're looking for things

are strategies which will help me with Trends then think again as it will not yield you a lot of results in the long run since trends are so hard to find. Understanding this concept will help you to prepare your mindset when it comes to the following protocol, which requires you to use patterns. Even though Trends can be hard to find, once you do find it and act on it correctly then the success rate will be very high. One thing to remember with any protocols but you require you to look at the trends, would be that you will need a lot of money to use a properly. This is because possession of a large amount of capital reduces the chances of you going down during an extended draw down. With that being said, let's talk about the three strategies which can help you tremendously to make a ton of money with Forex Trading.

Breakout

Breakout trend is a trend that you need to act on quickly to see amazing results, simply explain to you what a Breakout trend is it is when the market has suddenly gone up or down which could result in a new direction. Think of the breakout Trend as something which is just coming out, and you're guessing that it is going to be fantastic for currency there for you invest in it, most of the time it works amazingly. The only downfall will be that the breakout trend has no guarantee if it's going to turn into a trend or not. However, the great thing about the breakout trend is that you can come out of it as soon as possible. If you're full daytime trader, then you will know when the trading is going down, or the dollar is going up or down. Based on that judgment, you can pull out the money or keep going if the trend is going up or down. The great thing about the break out method would be that the market moves beyond the boundaries, meaning that you will achieve most likely new highs or new lows. Most of the time it is new highs, if there are a Currency Change chances are there is going to be a breakout. However, this isn't the case most of the time, so make sure before you get into the break out a method that you know for sure that it is going to go up. There is no sure way to find out that it is going to go up or not, however, based on your judgment and after some research, you should have a clear idea on how this trend is going to end up. Keeping that in mind, the breakout method could be an excellent way for beginners to start making some money as soon as possible. Many top forex traders recommend that beginner start with this trend, in our opinion it is a little bit on the risky side. However, any trend is going to be risky, and Forex Trading, in general, is dangerous as compared to having a full-time job.

Carry out trade

The carry trade method is not something many beginners follow. However it can be used by beginners to see amazing results. The way the special words as they bank on currencies dropping down and up. For example, a great carry out trade with be the Canadian and US dollar, the US dollar has always been high. However, there have been times when the Canadian dollar drops down very low and vice versa. When that happens, you know that you could trade your money and make more back depending on where you live. Many people have banked on the Canadian and US dollar to make this work for them in terms of profit. The great thing about the carry out method is that it is very calculated. However, it is based on trends are requires you to let your money sit for a long time. There are a lot of other ways to do the carry out trade. However, we will keep it very simple for you so you can understand how to follow the carryout trade

indeed and see the most benefit out of it. Keep in mind that the carryout rate is perhaps the safest trend-based method you can use to make more money. Overall, the only downfall with the carryout trade would be that you have to let your money sit for a long. Of time as compared to the break out method. However, once you do get the idea of how it is to be followed, you will be in a much better position and terms of making more money even if it is in the longer term.

Moving average crossover

This Forex strategy for beginners uses a simple moving average (SMA). SMA is an indicator which lags and uses older price data unlike other strategies, also tends to move more slowly than other ones. The longer the time which the SMA is averaged, the slower it moves. Often, top traders tend to use longer SMA with some shorter SMA. To explain to you how it works is that it looks at the lower prices and determines whether the new rates will be higher or not. This strategy is solely based on the trading system. If you are not getting better trading strategies, then chances are you will not see the results you are expecting from this method.

Research

Regardless of the investment that you make, be sure always to do your research. Doing research is a must. It is what will increase your chances of making the right investment decision. As the saying goes, "Knowledge is power." The more that you understand something, the more likely that you will be able to predict how it will move in the market. This is why doing research is essential. It will allow you to know if something is worth investing in or not. Remember that you are dealing with a continuously moving market, so it is only right that you keep yourself updated with the latest developments and changes, and the way to do this is by doing research.

Just because you have surfed the web for a few hours does not mean that you are already in the position to make an investment decision. You should understand that doing research should be part of your daily life as an investor/trader. Even if you are just a side trader, it is still essential that you do your research so that you will be informed of the best trading practices.

Remember that gaining information is not limited to just surfing the web for information. It is also suggested that you join online groups and forums that are related to your chosen investment. This way, you will be able to meet and connect with like-minded people. There is also a good chance that you can learn something from them.

Do not rush the process of doing research. Take note that you make decisions based on the information that you have on hand, and such information that you have will depend on the time and efforts that you put into doing research. Make sure that all of your decisions are backed up by solid research and analysis.

Write a Journal

Although not a requirement, writing a journal can be beneficial. You do not need to be a professional writer to write a memoir; however, you need to do two things: Update your journal regularly and be completely honest with everything that you write in your journal. By having a journal, you will be able to identify your strengths and weaknesses more effectively. It can also help you realize lessons that you might otherwise overlook.

You can record anything in your journal that is related to your business or investment. Ideally, it should contain your reasons, as well as your objectives. You can also write down your mistakes and new learnings that you encounter along the way.

In the first few weeks, you might not appreciate the value of keeping a journal. However, after some time, you will start to understand its importance, especially once you begin to notice your progress or developments. The important thing is to persist in writing your journal. It will allow you to view yourself from a new perspective, from a standpoint that is free from bias and prejudice.

Have a Plan

Whether you are going to start forex trading or trade in general, it is always good to have a plan. Make sure to set a clear direction for yourself. This is also an excellent way to avoid being controlled by your emotions or becoming greedy. You should have a short-term plan and a long-term plan. You should also be ready for any form of contingency. Of course, it is impossible to be prepared for everything. If you are suddenly faced with an unexpected and challenging situation, take your time to study the situation and develop a new plan. Never take action without proper planning. Poor planning leads to poor execution but having a good idea usually ends up favorably. You should stick to your plan. However, there are certain instances when you may have to abandon your project, such as when you realize that sticking to the same program will not lead to a desirable outcome or in case you find a much better idea. Proper planning can give you a sense of direction and ensure the success of execution.

Make your plans practical and reasonable. Remember that you ought to stick to whatever project you come up with, so be sure to keep your ideas real. Before you come up with an idea, you must first have quality information. Again, this is why doing research is very important.

What if you fail to execute your plan? This is not uncommon. If this happens to you, relax and think about what made you fail to stick to your plan? Was it favorable to you or not? Take some time to analyze the situation and learn as much as you can from it. Indeed, having a plan is different from executing it. It is more challenging to implement a plan as it demands that you take positive actions.

Learn from Your Competitors

Pay attention to your competitors and learn from them. Studying your competitors is also an excellent way to identify your strengths and weaknesses. You can learn a great deal from your competitors, especially ideas on how you can better improve your business.

Your competitors can also help you promote your trading goals and draw more techniques. This way, you get a better idea of how to trade. You do not have to fight against your competitors; you can work together.

It is prevalent for people online to support one another. , it is a good practice that you connect with other traders, especially those who are in the same niche. Do not think of them as your direct competitors, and you might be surprised just how friendly they can be.

Now, a common mistake is to consider yourself always better than the others. This is wrong as you are only deluding yourself, making you fail to see the bigger picture. Instead of still seeing yourself better than your competitors, learn from them, and see how you can use this knowledge to improve your trading endeavors

Cash-out

Some people who trade forex or invest in crypto currency commit the mistake of not making a withdrawal. The reason why they do not cash out is so that they can grow their funds. Since you can only earn a percentage of what you are trading/investing, having more funds in your account means that you can make a higher profit return. Although this may seem reasonable, it is not a recommended approach. It is strongly advised that you should request a withdrawal. You should understand that the only way to truly enjoy your profits is by turning them into cash; otherwise, it is only as if you were using a demo account. Also, by making a withdrawal, you get to lower your risks, since the funds that you withdraw will no longer be exposed to risks. You do not have to remove all your profits right away. If you want, you can withdraw 30% of your total profits, allowing the remaining 70% to add up to the funds in your account. The important thing is to make a withdrawal still now and then.

Take a Break and Have Fun

Making money online can be fun and exciting; however, it can also be a tiring journey. Therefore, give yourself a chance to take a break from time to time. When you take a break, do not spend that time thinking about your online business. Instead, you should spend it to relax your body and clear your mind. If you do this, then you will be more able to function more effectively. This is an excellent time to go on a vacation with your

family or friends or at least enjoy a movie night at home. Do something fun that will put your mind off of business for a while. Do not worry; after this short break, and you are expected to work even more.

Making money online is a long journey, so enjoy it. Making money online can be lots of fun. Do not just connect with people to build a good following, but also try to make friends with your connections. You do not have to take things too seriously. Keep it fun and exciting.

Chapter 14: Forex Analysis

Now that you are through with the basic elements that go into every single trade, it is time to delve further into the different strategies to use to determine the possible movements in the market. You must already be familiar with the different factors and forces that cause currencies to gain and lose value over time. This time we will explore the different analytical strategies to put this knowledge to good use. A lot of traders will take pieces of these strategies to formulate their own personalized approach in analyzing currency movement. What is important to know is that there are no perfect strategies, but some trading strategies do work better than others. It is up to you to determine which of these strategies will work for you and your trading comfort levels. Sometimes, even the best strategy will not work. You must not assume that the Forex market will never be beneficial, instead accept the fact that there will be ups and down when trading Forex.

Introduction to Analysis

Forex analysis can be thought of as being divided into two separate analytical schools of thought; fundamental analysis and technical analysis. Fundamental analysis mainly looks at the overall context of a currency, while technical analysis primarily focuses on raw and historical data. Fundamental analysis focuses on economic, political, and financial factors while a technical report focuses on charts, patterns, and other inherent movements.

Fundamental analysts mostly do not consider technical analysis as an effective way to determine the market's movement as they mainly look at the forces outside of the Forex market. The external factors that are primarily looked at are the different relationships of the countries and businesses that directly affect the exchange rates, which include the complex economics and macroeconomics of the factors that drive prices up and down. In contrast, technical analysts don't really pay attention to external forces and are mainly concerned with past rates and data, future trends, and recent patterns. For these types of traders, the Forex market is a self-contained ecosystem with internal factors that determine fluctuations dependent on the buying and selling of different currencies.

As an example, an increase in the value of the euro over the US dollar will be seen by a fundamental analyst as a result of specific changes with the relationship of the EU and the United States. They might also consider factors such as the countries' comparative interest rates and their respective inflations rates. Traders using this school of thought might also try to formulate an educated guess as to whether the trend would continue based on fundamental variables that can be ascertained from sources such as news reports, financial reports, and other predictive data. Technical analysts, on the other hand, will see the rise in the value of the euro to the US dollar as nothing more than a new uptrend. They will analyze both the current and past chart values and using various technical tools, analyze whether the trend will continue or return.

School of Thought Comparison

A lot of new traders would often ask the question, "Which is better?" Technical analysis and fundamental analysis both have their own advantages and disadvantages. The main reason for the divide is primarily because both types of analysis have proven track records of being somewhat accurate. Those who personally prefer fundamental analysis would argue that it has a superior efficacy because the movement in relation to economic data is observable. The connection between economics and the value of their respective currencies is undeniable, while in some cases the relationship may only become clear in hindsight. However, there are some cases where economic strife or improvements contradict market movements in very counterintuitive ways. In most cases, the underlying fundamental factors directly relate to significant currency movements. Traders that quickly jump on these movements, either by their own analysis or through someone else's conclusions, will tend to be greatly rewarded for their efforts.

Meanwhile, technical analysts argue that their method is much safer given that each trade is more specific and has the backing of large amounts of data. Trades using this particular method are every exact, and almost no emotional factor is at play. The types of patterns and data used in this method are quantifiable and observable, negating the need for speculation and argument. Unlike fundamental analysis, which might be up for debate or is subjective, raw data and chart patterns are more exact and concrete in technical analysis. Trades made through this method are only executed when all indicators are supportive of the final analysis.

The ace in the hole for technical analysts in the entire argument is the fact that technical analysis can be applied in almost all types of asset trading, including the stock market and securities market. Fundamental analysts would have to overhaul their previous trains of thought in these markets as they would have to learn its unique framework when compared to the Forex market. Technical analysts will have no problems jumping into these other types of markets given that the charts and patterns still work in the same way. A technical analyst that was previously trading commodities will have no problems jumping into the Forex market; although he or she would have to familiarize himself or herself with the peculiarities of the Forex market beforehand.

Fundamental Analysis

As previously mentioned, fundamental analysis will deal mostly with the external factors that affect the price of any particular currency. Certain factors are quantifiable, while others are qualitative. Some of the more concrete factors will involve economic and financial factors; this includes quarterly earnings reports and economy-related political movements. The more qualitative factors will involve developments in the realm of investor sentiments, political crisis, and other geopolitical developments. Fundamental analysis is sometimes referred to by traders as a complicated art form to master, as it will require a lot of investigative and analytical skills to piece together different factors that will ultimately result in a robust forecast. There are a lot of competing narratives that will often confuse fundamental analysts, but those that can read into the situation will more often than not come up with the best forecasts.

Global Interest Rates and Inflation

Global interest rates play a significant part in the movements within the Forex market. It can also be said that global interest rates rule the Forex market. A specific currency's interest rate determines its perceived value as much as its actual value compared to other currencies. Fundamental analysts closely track and look at each country's central bank and its respective monetary policies. Each country has its own central bank. The United States has the Federal Reserve, the UK has the Bank of England, Switzerland has the Swiss National Bank, the EU has the European Central Bank, and Australia has the Reserve Bank of Australia, and so on.

The main determining factor for the rise and fall of interest rates in any given country is to maintain price stability and control inflation. Inflation is the increase in the prices of goods and services within a country. The sustained increase is closely related to the purchasing power of a country's currency. Hence, inflation is inevitable and is part of a growing economy. A country's central bank will need to control its country's inflation through the adjustment of its currency's interest rate. Too much inflation will directly harm the economy as a whole, and central banks will have to find a way to keep it at a comfortable level to sustain an acceptable growth rate. An increase in interest rates will lower overall growth, while at the same time slow down the country's inflation rate. This happens because businesses will now borrow less money, which will, in turn, prevent their establishments from growing. In contrast, when interest rates are lowered, more businesses will borrow money, boosting expansion, capital spending, and economic growth.

A currency's interest rate will determine how much capital will be going in and out of a certain country. Investors are more inclined to place their money in countries with higher interest rates, thus increasing the demand for that country's currency. The higher the demand, the stronger a currency becomes when compared to other currencies. This also works inversely; when a country's interest rate is low, demand for its currency decreases. This makes that country's currency weaker when compared to other currencies. Fundamental analysts consider these interest rates when trading different currency pairs.

In most cases, interest rates don't change a lot, and changes don't happen very often. Interest rates also don't make drastic movements, which means that if a currency's interest rates have dropped significantly over a long period, it will likely increase again at some point. The key here is to try to determine the direction of the interest rates of a particular currency.

One way of determining the direction of a particular pair's movement using interest rates is through a technique called "interest rate differential." This method typically involves the comparison between one currency's interest rate to the interest rate of its paired currency. The difference between the interest rates is what fundamental analysts look at to determine possible shifts in the prices of the currency. When the interest rates of two currencies move in opposite directions, a significant movement is likely going to happen. That's pretty much about Global Interest Rates and Inflation.

Economic Indicators

Economic factors calculate the statistical information of the country's economy. The economic indicators preview the patterns, performance, and future predictions of an economy. As beginners, you must understand that economic indicators have a massive impact on trading. If you don't understand economic indicators, trading might become complicated. The leading factors of financial systems links with economic indicators. Each indicator differs as per the target group, origin, and on various markets. The indicators are divided by region so that it's convenient to handle and understand, so such divisions are European indicators, Asian indicators, and US indicators. Economic indicators and surveys are often released. However, due to the advancement of technology, anyone can access economic data and indicators whenever they want. As Forex traders, you must understand the impact created by economic indicators on the Forex market. You must analyze them to make a proper decision in trading. So, more important indicators that you must know include:

Interest rates

Unemployment rate

Changes in the Gross Domestic Product (GDP)

Consumer Price Index (Inflation)

Employee Cost Index (ECI)

165

Purchasing Managers Index (PMI)

Producer Price Index (PPI)

Federal funds rate

Income

Beige Book

Balance of Trade

Mutual Fund Flows

Corporate Profits

Business Outlook Survey

Currency Strength

Consumer Credit Report

Wholesale Trade Report

Durable Goods Report

Employment Situation Report

Industrial Production

Money Supply

Productivity Report

Retail Sales Report

However, you must understand that frequencies of indicators will differ monthly, weekly, or even daily. Only after proper speculation, economic indicators are updated, and Forex and other traders make sure to be up-to-date with speculations. All their trading moves will be based on speculations. When you look at an economic situation, it will have an impact when announced and during the speculation. Both situations will create a shift in the Forex market. For example, when a government issues building permits, there will be more jobs, when there are more jobs, the unemployment rate will reduce. Hence, the consumption rate will increase while resulting in strengthening the value of local currency. Let me put it simply, and an economic indicator will provide the information that a trader needs when understanding the things happening in the economy. If you consider the U.S. economy, it is a happening economy. You will not be able to predict that easily; hence, economic indicators are important to get a good understanding of the market. However, you will come across lagging indicators as well as coincident indicators.

Different traders use economic indicators in different ways. However, to benefit from economic indicators, you must focus on market analysis. You can do primary research or consider analyses, and the choice is yours. For example, when a trader is aware of the event to be taken place, he or she will speculate the market. Based on it, the trader will select a certain instrument to Forex trade. The trader must anticipate the trade properly if he or she wants to acquire substantial profit. When you are speculating the economic indicators, it is important to know about financial events, markets, and all the general factors that will have an impact on the economic indicators. If you are through with these details, your speculation will be firm.

As a beginner, you must become comfortable with using the economic calendar and learn how it links to economic indicators. Once you understand it, you'll get a clear view of its impact on Forex trading. If you utilize economic indicators successfully, you'll be able to achieve success in Forex trading, and you'll learn to manage your expectations as well.

Anyway, before you utilize economic indicators, you must use the information accordingly to match with the context. Of course, raw data is valuable, but you must be vigilant to use it. Luckily, you are benefitted from the profit groups and different governments because they conduct surveys to provide information to the traders. On the other hand, if you try to do it on your own, you won't be able to do it as successfully as profit groups and different governments.

If you want to trade Forex successfully, you must have an economic calendar with the updated information. If you have the economic calendar, it is easy to include all the essential releases and events that will impact the Forex market. For beginners, an economic calendar is one of the most useful tools because it helps to identify the market moves. You can use the forecasted and the actual values to make proper decisions in trading.

You can select a few indicators and master it so that you'll be able to use it successfully when making a trading decision. But, it doesn't mean you can't use all the indicators in trading. Anyway, the choice is in your hand as per your understanding. But remember, you will never find that magic indicator that tells you to trade because there isn't any. It is you who has to use the indicators carefully to benefit from trading.

Debt

Forex debt is something that is unnecessary because naïve traders fall into debts deliberately. Most naïve traders assume high leverage will bring them higher profits. But, when you handle with high leverage even without prior experience, you are pushing yourself to a dangerous situation. Hence, before you begin live trading, you must use a demo account to become familiar with the market. It's apparent that a higher percentage of novice traders lose money because they ignore the logical factors. They are aware that trading a live account without experience will lead to debts, yet they are greedy to make money.

If you think Forex is simple so that you can make easy money, you've got it wrong. Most naïve traders end up facing huge financial losses because they don't have the capital to cover up their losses. However, the underlying problem with Forex debt is greed and improper risk management. If the trader is greedy, he or she may even try to benefit from the last pip. But, one can avoid greed by expanding their vision about market opportunities. And the next is improper risk management, so for this, you must learn the risk management concept before you begin live trading. Even a professional trader must understand risk management to protect the Forex account.

But, if you are already in debt, you must try to save some money to increase your capital. Of course, it will take some time, but you can do it!

Politics

Most beginners don't understand the Forex market. Even though they know about fluctuations in the currency value, they do not know how the currency value has fluctuated. Many factors including politics affect price fluctuation, and naïve traders don't spend the time to understand this overwhelming process. If a country is facing a war, it will have a huge impact on the country's currency value. Basically, political factors may affect a country's currency value positively or negatively. The effect will be based on the war situation of the country. Yet, currency exchange will have some differences. As beginners, you must keep an eye on this! But, remember, stable countries gain more recognition than the countries that don't prevail in peace. Likewise, numerous political factors impact the Forex market.

Hence, as traders, you have to keep your eyes open to the changes.

Psychology

Psychology is a huge part of Forex trading. Most professional traders emphasize the importance of psychology in trading. Some professionals believe it is more important than academic knowledge. When we consider the trading mistakes, the basement for the highest number of mistakes would be psychology. Traders are humans, so no wonder that psychology is taking a toll on humans. The constant mistakes are directly related to the psychology of traders.

Different emotions act as a barrier to naïve traders. For example, fear is one of the emotions that constantly attack naïve traders. Even if the trader is confident in trading, it will be hard to make up the mind to enter into trade and the reason is fear. In this case, the trader will be wasting a lot of time trading the demo account. Hence, fear has a huge impact on trading.

Of course, human minds look for the safer option, but in trading, you have to handle risks to reach the top. If you are pulling yourself away from entering into a trade, it means you're pulling yourself from the chances of earning profits.

No matter what others say, you will not be able to avoid the trading fear unless you try to avoid it on your own. For that, you must make an effort to understand the trading psychology in detail. But, let me tell you. If you know your weakness, it is more than enough to become successful. If you know that you fear entering new trades, you can work on it and improve your trading behaviors. But, think about the ones who don't know what's going wrong in their trading style. Of course, they will keep on trading until they blow their account completely. Hence, if you know your weakness, you will overcome soon!

Charts

Initially, reading the charts can be confusing, but over time you'll understand. There are different displays as per the price displayed. The Japanese candlesticks are the most common price method considered by most traders. However, candlestick charts are preferred on the Forex chart because it is easier to read. When you are reading the charts, you must use the patterns to understand the price and the market movement. If you don't prefer this, you can opt for line charts. You can find the closing price when you use the line chart. Or you can opt for a bar chart which is just like the candlestick chart. When you make use of the bar chart, you will be able to find the price opened and closed in the Forex market.

The best thing is you can use the technical analysis to read Forex charts. Even if you don't prefer technical analysis, you can benefit from it when you are using it on Forex charts. You can include technical analysis of your charting system because it is allowed by most systems. Yet, try to get the best out of the technical analysis when you have difficulties in identifying the price. Anyway, you must remember that keeping things simple is the best way to trade successfully.

So, there we end Forex analysis. But remember, learning Forex is a continued journey so the more you learn, the more you find!

Conclusion

Contrary to what every Forex 'expert' out there would have you believe, it's not easy to learn how to trade Forex at all. Trading Forex is one of the most challenging skills you can ever set out to learn, which is especially daunting if you're a beginner just starting out to learn how to trade Forex. If you're finding it hard to learn how to trade Forex successfully right now, you're probably wondering: "Can a beginner make money in Forex trading?" By the end of this article, you'll know what you can do to make money in Forex trading right now.

Can A Beginner Make Money In Forex Trading?

If you have a look around the many Forex websites, forums, seminars and magazines, it seems like everyone's making millions of dollars trading Forex! The thing is, Forex traders love to talk about their winning trades and make themselves out to be wildly profitable traders, but the reality is that only 5% of Forex traders are consistently making money. Yes, even a beginner can make money in Forex trading, but there's a big difference between making money in Forex and making a full time income, achieving financial freedom, and building wealth through Forex.

What Stops Beginners From Making An Income

So what's stopping beginners from making a consistent, long term income from trading Forex? Well, unlike the professional Forex traders working for the big banks and hedge funds, most beginner traders learning to trade Forex aren't paid a full time salary to immerse themselves in the markets. If you're just starting out in Forex, then you've probably got a full time job that you spend at least 8 hours a day on, and a family and social life outside of that. That means that you have a very real shortage of time to get yourself to the level where you can trade like a pro, and believe me, it takes a lot of time and consistent effort.

It takes years of study, practice and real experience in the markets to learn how to trade Forex successfully, and get to the level where you can consistently make money in Forex trading. Not to mention that you'll be taking on, for all intents and purposes, an unpaid part time job that will chain you to your computer while you are trading. It's something that will alienate you from your social circle, and put considerable strain on your family relationships as well. It's no wonder that most traders wanting to learn how to trade Forex will give up within 3 months, and never make money in Forex trading.

What You Can Do To Make Money In Forex Trading Now

So what can you do to make money in Forex trading right now? The best shortcut I know is to buy a proven Forex trading system to do your trading for you. I'm not going to look you in the eye and tell you that you can just go out there and pick any system and make millions, because that's simply not true. Profitable trading systems are rare, and you need to choose very carefully. That said, if you can find a trading system that works, you can overcome the biggest challenges any trader faces while they learn how to trade Forex. You'll be able to gain valuable Forex market experience, preserve your personal relationships and most importantly make money in Forex trading while you learn how to trade Forex.

When you've built up the capital and income of your Forex systems operation, and have gathered up valuable trading experience, you may decide to try out trading Forex for yourself. Regardless of whether you trade with an automatic Forex system in the short, medium or long term, it's a powerful solution that will enable you to make money in Forex trading even if you're a beginner.

www.ingramcontent.com/pod-product-compliance
Lightning Source LLC
Chambersburg PA
CBHW071226210326
41597CB00016B/1961